A VISIT HOME

A Collection of Short Stories

A Sketch

And

A Few Poems

By

John Dingley
with a contribution by
Cassie Powell

John Dingley

Published by Gwenwst Books 2016

19 Oakley Avenue #3

St Paul, MN 55104

Cover design by Dan Sexton.

Manufactured in the United States of America

Library of Congress Registration (Pending)

ISBN 978-0-9914423-2-4

Ebook ISBN 978-09914423-3-1

DEDICATION

This book is dedicated to the memory of Jeffrey Jones Powell, Tremaen, a man who loved to laugh and to make others laugh. He also loved the story, a tale well told. His daughter Cassie wrote this after his death in 2014.

Dad

Stumbled words,
A whispered cry,
The sad truth,
I have to say goodbye.

A solid heart,
An honest thought,
The memories,
I will have to sort.

A funny man,
With words so wise,
My love for you,
I'll never hide...

But you will live on,
Within our thoughts,
True memories
And lessons you taught.

Will miss you Dad
That much is true.
But a happy girl,
That my Dad was YOU.

See you in the morning DAD.

Not too early mind!

ACKNOWLEDGEMENTS

We can have great ambitions to do all sorts of things great and small and in my case little is accomplished without the help and encouragement from the people in my life. They follow.

My sisters Snowy and Jane, who, encourage me to stick at it on a regular basis, inspiring, when considering the distance between Mid Wales and the Mid West.

I have to especially thank Liz Williams, Alltmawr, who insisted all those years ago that I should write. I don't want to stop, now.

To Bob Anderson who was looking forward to this work until his death. He died too young.

My good friend Richard Meredith, always there to verify, and encourage my efforts.

Eric and Brita and their wonderful children, Claire and Francis. Eileen Kerr, Jordan and Dan Chariper, Erin Hart, Kathy Luby, Gary Smith, Eirwen and Church, Sadie Jenkins, Sally Evans, Emily Darling, Teresa McCormick, Tom Dahill and Ginny Johnson.

To Amy Ries, John Howe and my fellow Raptor Resource Project board members.

A special thank you to Craig Anderson, Decorah, and Tom Tulien, Minneapolis, who generously keep the roofs over my head.

"Madam Librarian" Kristen Torresdal, Decorah Library.

To Gail Whitney for editorial advice.

Patrick O'Donnell who story and copy edited this work.

Jordan Chariper for the front cover photographs.

Richard Meredith for the Red Lion picture on the back cover.

Teresa McCormick for the mug shot.

Dan Sexton for cover design.

The Celtic Collaborative, and its work to further the literary and performance potential of the Minnesota Celtic Community

Finally, members of the Midwest Independent Publishers Association, particularly Sybil Smith of Smith House Press, who teaches and guides all writers who contact her on their journey to self publication. She has always been available for advice.

CONTENTS

POEMS

A

VISIT HOME

John

Dingley

INTRODUCTION

What follows is an eclectic collection of stories, poems and a simple sketch.

The stories have been experienced or collected over the years and are based in truth or the wild imaginings of storytelling individuals that show up in the unlikeliest of places. Humour has always been the goal of the stories and many of them have been used in my one man show.

The comic sketch was written for the Na Fianna Theatre, Irish Players, and was performed in Chicago and the Twin Cities.

Cassie Powell is my niece and I am honoured to include some of her work here.

The poems in general are the results of a more serious take on the world, its life and its people.

My writing has evolved over the years, as it should. However, while living in America it has become a hybrid of both British and American English. Readers from specific sides of the Atlantic will notice this. Separating the two has become an almost practical impossibility.

As you the reader wind your way through the twists and turns of this work you will inevitably come across words, place names and other odd things that will need some explanation or translation. Some of these have been explained. However, the portal to the World Wide Web should lead you to clarification of many of the others. Look things up and who knows you might find the adventures herein much expanded by additional research.

A VISIT HOME

Builth Wells is a market town that devises ways to sell itself without the collective knowledge of its happy residents. Tourists do visit in a state of being lost on their way to somewhere else or in an equally frustrating state of wishing they were lost when they get there. And all that is lost through its year, whether it be people, business or sunny weather, often stays lost.

However for four days in July, agriculture pays a visit, growing crops of people, harvested from fields of automotive pandemonium. Ejecting the exploring contents into local hostelries in the same manner that viruses invade the DNA of cells, often with insidious motives, although the cellular watering holes dotted along the arterial streets instigate rambunctious pleasures.

The town is actually a crossroads of twisted, mangled, confusingly integrated highways that have avoided any resemblance to a crossroads in the mind's eye. A mini conurbation that is as mysteriously adventurous as any that could be found in places a hundred times as large. Alongside these meandering byways is that rugby player laden, Groe Green, a meadow, devoid of grazing bulls and bordered by a sylvan, conker shrouded footpath revealing between its robust trunks a sparkling river Wye. There it is the straightest, salmon swimming, rush of water of its length, riffling its un-lost way through one way streets.

Even though in its history there is said to have been a momentary lapse into treachery that brought about the separation of a royal head from a noble Welsh Prince's body; its later, better known, fame came along in the Chalybeate waters of its spas. Taking the waters seemed to be a diversionary activity for those individuals who regularly indulged in Gin and Quinine to avoid Malaria, when on visits to foreign parts.

It is to this town that I would return after a five year absence in foreign parts myself. Not to take the odorous waters, but to visit memorable friends and relatives. So from that Mississippi-straddling, twin town conurbation of Minneapolis and St Paul, I set forth to celebrate the end of year in indulgent, holiday activities, accompanied by three American friends looking for unusual cultural experiences. Fortunately for them and others on similar excursions the serendipity of Celtic Countries and Character rarely disappoints.

The travelers were Tom, who I worked with building stone fireplaces and other structures during the summers. Tom's daughter also came along and Marni a talented beauty and provider of liquid indulgences in a bar called "The 617 Club". We were all accommodated by my parents in the spacious farm house that was once my home. I was asked to be the guide into the depths of Welsh scenery and culture.

The Wednesday before Christmas, Tom and I found ourselves promenading the main streets ready to insert ourselves into the DNA of Builth Wells watering holes. A few feet from the front door of the White Horse Inn our ears were assaulted by the ringing of a loud bell. Pulling up alongside was a bright red fire engine. It stopped, the window was lowered and then I heard a familiar voice.

"John, I thought that we had gotten rid of you."

There leaning through the window in an 'on the way to a fire', full uniform was David, head of the local, volunteer fire department. Before leaving Wales I had worked with the, sometimes, volatile David for several years.

"Where are you going?" He asked.

I was more interested in where he might be going. Was there a fire? A quick observation told me that there was no fire, because David was the only flame fighting individual on board. I replied, "my American friend Tom and I were about to go in here," I pointed to the hole in the wall of the White Horse, "to have one."

A huge grin appeared on his face. "Well, hang on, I will join you and pay some attention to dousing the fire in my throat."

In full fire fighting uniform David joined us in the bar and bought a cheerful round of the world's finest Bitter Ale. A catch-up conversation ensued. Although, Tom was taking part in the liquefied expressions he seemed preoccupied and unnoticed to David, was looking the uniformed man up and down with what seemed like incredulity.

There was less than half a pint left in the glasses of the fire drenching liquid when Freddie the local postman, in his Royal Mail uniform, came through the door to drop on the end of the bar the pubs correspondence.

"John! You are back from America. Are you back for good?"

David responded first, as a fireman would to a three alarm blaze. "No! He is back for no good."

"Well, by damned," said Freddie, "this calls for a pint."

Money was laid out for more pints. Fire in throats would be soaked completely out of existence.

Tom's flames of incredulity had now been fanned further as he looked up and down Freddie's royal livery. Only a few more gulps of celebration were taken before Tom could contain his liquid curiosity no longer. "Can you guys do this?"

David's answer was the first to emerge from the two inquiring faces. "Do what?"

"Well, you are both working and are in uniform. Is it legal for you to drink while you are working?"

Big smiles crept onto the faces above those proudly worn uniforms. David responded again. "Legal, legal. If we want to stop and have a drink we can. It's not as if we are not getting our work done."

Tom looked at Freddie. "Your post office allows you to do this?"

"Well, I haven't had any complaints, yet. This time of year I might have a drink in every pub I deliver to. I get all the letters delivered, mind. I haven't missed yet. There has been once or twice when I was close to legless getting back to the depot at this festive time of year, but I have always got the job done."

Tom seemed to be stunned as he turned to David. "What if there was a fire?"

"That's easy. If the siren went off I would have time to finish my pint before climbing aboard the engine. I would drive off with bells ringing and by the time I was at the top of the street all the volunteers would be on board and it would be the fastest turn out of the year."

The pints were soon emptied and conversations shortened as the two uniformed men went back to their work. Tom and I continued our journey up the main street to visit another important, watering hole, "The Barley Mow".

Marni had asked if I could arrange for her to serve liquid indulgences across a Welsh bar. The Barley Mow was an ideal venue for polishing up international relations, this market towns favorite for livestock men to celebrate or drown the disappointment of an animal sale. We were welcomed by John the landlord. I proposed the opportunity of employing, for one evening, a professional mixologist from the land of lakes.

His first response was. "Can she pull a decent pint?"

She might have been able to mix drinks with skilled aplomb, but in Wales the consummate skill required to indulge the masses was pulling the "perfect pint". I smiled. "Don't you worry, she is a fast learner. A tutorial from an experienced pint puller like your self will have her up to par in about four minutes."

He contemplated for a few seconds. "Alright, then, bring her in by six tomorrow and I will give her the job for the evening."

At a few minutes to six on the Thursday, Marni was delivered and duly indulged for three or four minutes in the art of producing "perfect pints".

John was suited up in his best and sported an expression of impending pleasure and relaxation. I looked him over. "Boy, you've dressed up for this, haven't you?"

"Aye, if she is going behind there," he pointed at the bar, "then I am going out for the evening. I haven't had a day off for six months." He turned for the door and left Marni in full charge of the entire establishment.

She pulled Tom and I two perfect halves and was soon working the bar with the professional flourish that would impress even the most discriminating customer.

As there was a girl friend from my past holding forth behind the bar of "The Swan" another well known hostelry, across the street, Tom and I drank up and left Marni in full command. She objected to our leaving, however we left anyway and crossed the street.

The Swan's main room was elongated, with an 'L' shaped bar that was splashed with four men, almost equally spaced, possibly in more ways than one, peacefully perched on barstools sipping their bitter ale, the relish of its flavor much diminished after many refills. We were served by Ann and inserted ourselves into this seemingly normal scene on a pair of stools close to the main door.

Within ten minutes the door burst open creating a bluster of cool air that carried along with it a small woman, who had the initial showings of unkempt hair and clothes. In her hands she carried a steaming-hot, pleasantly, aromatic dinner and a knife and fork. The Swan didn't serve food on Thursdays, only at weekends and on Mondays when the auctioneer's mallet came down selling flocks of sheep and small herds of cattle.

The determined woman briskly homed in on a lone man at the far end of the bar. The way she moved quickly focused the attention of everyone else in the room. She arrived at her destination and banged the dinner down onto the bar in front of the man and laid down the knife and fork by its side. It was then that she spoke with a very unpracticed, crippling, soprano voice. "You left the 'ouse this morning to go and find work and where did you come to? This bloody pub. Well, you might as well eat your dinner here." She turned and just as briskly left the building leaving the rest of us surrounded by the remnants of the cool air.

The man, undoubtedly the husband of the woman, calmly picked up the knife and fork and proceeded to eat the dinner as if it was a routine occurrence. Of course, for all Tom and I knew it could have been.

Just as the air had calmed and warmed the door burst open once again and another rush of cool air brought in a second small woman, who carried no dinner. She marched right up to a bachelor farm labourer that I had known in the years before my exit from the community. In a harsh, hardened, demanding voice she spoke. "Get off your stool."

At first he didn't even consider that this woman was addressing him. She repeated the demand. Only this time it was interspersed with flowery obscenities.

That seemed to get his attention. "What's the matter with you, woman?" He asked, in a deep baritone voice.

The woman's demand was repeated once more, however this time it was coupled with a claw like grip around the man's ear, her nails penetrating his flesh. Before he could object again she had flung him off the bar stool onto his back on the floor. All the open mouthed observers in the room expected her to jump on top of him, no doubt to punish him for some crime that was yet to be revealed. Instead she grabbed the barstool by its legs, picked it up and marched out the door with it muttering more obscenities, and words of violent intention toward someone who was lurking somewhere in the shadows, beyond the open door.

Before we could absorb what had just occurred a man charged in through the door and grabbed my barstool by its legs. It was not my property; however for the short time I had use of it I felt that it was and should be defended at all costs. I grabbed the seat of it and it soon became obvious that I was dueling with a man as if he were a lion and I was his whip-less tamer. The tussling lasted for a few moments when he gave up on his endeavor and charged back out through the door. In seconds the entry way into the bar filled up with a brawl of people including the bar stool. Fists were being thrown. Painful, crippling grappling's, usually only committed by "all in" wrestlers were being carried out. Shirts were being torn off to reveal scratches and bite marks of a mouth that had all but a few of its teeth remaining. The police arrived and busied themselves with the task of unraveling the crude, pugilistic mass of what could be barely called civilized examples of humanity. They were arrested and removed and the barstool was returned to the man that had been thrown off it. He was, with his now blooded ear, still in the process of regaining an upright stance on shocked, shaky legs.

We were about to settle down again when another person entered and announced the latest news of the dueling masses of Builth Wells. "Boys." He said. "You should have seen the fight that broke out in the Barley Mow."

Suddenly I felt as if I had been in the middle of this battle and had received an almost mortal wound from that barstool itself. "Come on Tom," I said, "we had better go and see if Marni has survived this altercation."

We drank up quickly and scurried across the street and entered the Barley Mow. Everything seemed serene and normal. People were happily chatting while others played darts.

A man who I knew came up to me. "John, boy, I will tell you now. That Yank gel is the best. A fight broke out, you see and a glass was broken. She came out from behind the bar with a broom to sweep it up, however the fight had intensified. Bottles and furniture were being thrown around and as quick as a flash the broom became her peacemaker. In a few seconds she had beaten the whole of the combative mess out the door where they continued their war in the street."

Tom had half a grin on his face as he shook his head with disbelief. "Does this happen a lot here?"

"Once in awhile," I replied, "but I have never seen anything like that before."

The following Monday was Christmas Eve and market day in town. From one end to the other the town was a hustling, bustling, humming, happy place. People were everywhere, food supplies for the holidays and the week were being purchased along with last minute gift buying. In the market, animals were being sold at a brisk, urgent pace being cashed in to provide extra money; adequate funds for the celebrations was essential.

Every pub was full of happy voices, and many of those voices would explode into song, carols, hymn tunes and half remembered, operatic choruses. For those lost visitors exploring the confusion of activity the realization would quickly develop, Wales indeed, was a land of song.

A wide eyed Tom and I found ourselves in the Swan once more. It was not the quiet sparsely populated place we had visited before with interruptions of violent excitability. It was jammed full of people like a large flock of tightly packed sheep in a market pen. The song draped, bleating voices crowded the air above our heads. It was where everybody wanted to be. However, every cellular pub in those arterial streets was equally bursting at the seams with musical vigor and passion.

We lodged ourselves wedge like into this pubs expanded population, close to the door. Not that we were ready to leave or even in need of an escape route in case a bar stool duel was to break out. It was the easiest place to get served and to catch up on events past and present with old friends, interrupted every few minutes, when a man in the far reaches of the room would pitch a tune that would ignite all other voices throughout the entire bleating crowd like a magical, musical wave.

No women were delivering dinners to their husbands; however the human traffic was constant with the influx increasing when a familiar tune could be heard from the pub on the street.

Between two of the tunes, "Cwm Rhondda" and "We'll Keep a Welcome", a portly man in a smart three piece suit entered. He was supported at his elbow by a much younger man; a necessary precaution as the older man was well on his way to happy inebriation. It was Reg, a local dairy farmer, who sold his milk around the town. He saw me and his cheerful, rosy face lit up. "John, by damned, boy, it is good to see you. Back from America, are you?"

"Just for a visit, Reg."

"Well, you had better have a drink with me, now. I still have all the cows I bought from you before you left. Damned good stock, boy, damned good stock."

I introduced him to Tom and vice versa. "Tom this is Reg, he used to be the Mayor of Builth Wells."

As he shook Tom's hand he blurted out. "I am again. I am the mayor this very day and I am on my Christmas rounds. That reminds me. Just a minute." He moved closer to the bar still being supported by the young man. He removed his wallet and ordered drinks for everyone in the room.

Tom watched intently and turned to me. "You gotta be kidding me. That guy is the mayor?"

"Yes, and he will buy drinks for everyone in every pub in town."

Tom was skeptical and went on an extensive journey through the crowd to verify these new revelations. He returned convinced, that yes, Reg was the, generous, mayor of Builth Wells.

The New Year passed in Wales as it does around our planet and we returned to the frozen Mississippi's straddling, twin towns. It was four months later when Tom and I visited a friend of his who asked about his trip to Europe.

Tom smiled. "I went to Wales with John and stayed in his home and I will tell you now that John's home town is a drinking man's paradise."

This was a huge surprise to me. He had never mentioned this observation before.

He continued. "If you are a drinking man it would be your ideal home. If you are on your way to work or a man delivering the mail or even on your way to extinguish a fire in a bright red truck you can stop at any pub of your choice and have a drink and no one will do anything to stop you. If you want to spend the day at your favorite watering hole you don't have to worry about your meals. Your wife will deliver them to you right in the bar. When there are disputes they settle them by duking it out in the streets with barstools. Now, let me tell you this. You might think that we have a great democracy in this country, our 'land of the free', well you should think again. John's home town has perfected the democratic process. They pick the richest drunk in town and make him mayor."

WALES

I come home to Wales where wisdoms wit will sing,
Where in the eyes and throats there is a culture well enthroned.

The hiraith for the hwyl is the ship in which I move
Maintains my life, beating all its storms, and rarely lets me down.

There should always be a nowhere to move my Country's soul
Or its delicate, vibrant heart will never keep its place.

As her people move and travel through many other lands
Their soul is anchored in the mountains of a place that's always home.

The hardships of their lives, fall to the humor of the spirit.
They manifest god like power in the cradle of their hearts.

When native battle lines are drawn they use not the arms of war.
It is Eisteddfodau, where gallant seats and ribbons are the spoils of victory.

No oppression could break their backs, from other nations bold.
They allowed them in and diminished them with a smiling eye of strength.

For there the tongue of native voice holds out against that airy English noise.
For the Welsh words way takes the stand in their every pages nook.

Oh, should I know the language, pure, of my land among the hills
I would skillfully entangle it and conjure up a chair.

Translations. Hiraith = longing, Hwyl = spiritual high, Eisteddfod = competition for the arts. Each year at the National Eisteddfod the winning poet, bard, in the Welsh language, is chaired. To win the chair is Wales highest honour.

A COW IS LOOSE

The call came at three in the morning. It woke me up and I answered without a clue as to who it might be. "Hello!"

The voice at the other end asked if it was me. I said, "yes, it is."

It continued. "This is the University of Minnesota police. Are you the person who deals with the livestock on the St Paul campus?"

"I am."

"Oh, good, we have a problem. There is a cow loose and we are not sure where it came from and we are concerned that it may get out onto a highway. Could you come here and help us deal with it. Every time we get close it runs away."

"I shall be there in twenty minutes."

The reason I got this call was because I was the chief livestock attendant for the University of Minnesota, Department of Animal Science. My job, between classes, was to move beef cattle, sheep and pigs to various locations on the campus for livestock evaluation classes and for any other reasons that the professors came up with. I was given access to a tractor and trailer for this purpose. The job came with a bonus, I was the only undergraduate student to get a desk, and a phone, while on the campus.

Within the twenty minutes I arrived on the campus. I pulled up behind three police cars that were parked opposite Peters Hall where an Angus cow was peacefully grazing. The first car was a University car that contained two officers, male and female. The second was a St Paul City police car that contained two male officers. The third contained one officer and he was the Chief of Police for the University.

I got out of my old battered car and was quickly surrounded by the five officers. "Are you the livestock man?"

"Yes, I am."

"There's the cow over there. We have no idea where she might be from."

I pointed out that she was from the Beef Barn which was just up the street. "I will go and put her back." I made a move toward the animal and the officers were right there waving their arms and shouting except for one, who had his hand on his gun. It quickly became obvious that not one of these officers had had any experience with livestock.

This was not going to work. It seemed to me in America, that enthusiastic gung ho was all that a person needed to qualify as a police officer instead of careful thought and deliberate moves. I turned and raised my hands. "Please, I will do this by myself. You will only frighten her into running away."

"She has already done that." Said one.

I smiled. "I want you to stand back and stay quiet and I will put her back in the barn." They watched me go over to the cow and place my hand on her rump. She had been grazing for some time and was as full as a tic. "Come on, girl," I said, "let's get you to bed."

She walked at a steady cow's pace in front of me while my hand rested on her back. She stopped at the Beef Barn gate, contentedly chewing her cud, while I walked in front of her to open it. She entered and I closed it behind her. When I turned away, the job being completed, I was faced with a row of uniformed wide open mouths. I could see it going through their minds. "This guy must be some kind of cow whisperer."

One of them spoke. "Did you know that cow?"

I answered. "No, I didn't. I might have seen her in the barn from time to time."

The chief smiled. "Well, that was amazing. We could have never done what you just did ourselves. How can we ever thank you?"

What an opportunity. I quickly pointed out that as this occurs once in a while, particularly during the busy daylight hours when the livestock is more likely to be moved around it was not always easy for me to attend to the problem. I continued, "While here I have to park on the State Fair Grounds and having to go there can delay the animal's apprehension considerably."

The chief smiled, we were approaching the cars. "I think we can solve that problem for you." He pointed to my car.

"This is your car, I take it?"

"Yes, it is not much but, it gets me around."

He smiled. "Excellent." He took a note book out of his pocket and jotted down the registration number. "I will get your number distributed to all the officers and from now on you may park wherever you wish on campus as long as you are not disrupting traffic. You won't even have to plug meters. After all, we will want you right there when something escapes."

This was marvelous. If I was late getting to a class I would drive up over the curb and park on the lawn outside the building. The car would not be touched.

One day I was approached by the Dean of the College of Agriculture himself. He asked me if the old car he had seen parked illegally all over campus was mine. Naturally I answered, "Yes."

"Don't you ever get a ticket?"

I told him the full story, which he thoroughly enjoyed and then he turned and began to walk away and then stopped and turned back and looked me right in the eye. "Do you realize, you have better parking privileges than I do and I am the Dean of this campus?"

One fine spring day I had left the car parked on a strip of grass outside the Beef Barn and when I returned there was the familiar red striped, law enforcement, ticket under the wiper. Immediately, I assumed that there must be a new officer on patrol who had not been informed about my parking privileges.

I picked up the ticket and there was a hand written note attached. It read. "Hi, we don't mind you parking all over campus wherever you want, but you do have to renew your registration tabs."

LUTHER

His shuffling, turned down, rubber booted feet lead him into town.
A favorite pub and ale is usually his goal.
On important days you will find him in the market place
Droving sheep and cattle under auction's hammer.
The work is done and the bit of change is earned
And the Barley Mow is open and once again is gained.
A pint is soon within his grasp its foaming head his smile
And his knowing mind an ear for all of gossip's news.
Few, if ever, notice him his person to acknowledge,
Yet on his back a fluorescent coat to keep his journey safe.

The night again has filled the path that leads him to his home
And on his back the coat is lit by the lamps of those on wheels.
His head and belly full, his way is stretched again.
The addled mixture in his mind will take him through the night.
When those shuffled steps meander and from the path he strays
He brightens in the headlights so they can give him room.
They do not arrest the inebriate man in the market town of Builth.
He must wear a night bright coat to make himself standout.
For his night time glows are the means to his abode,
Although, Luther's brightness in the night is a better guide to us.

A WORLD OF OPTIMISM

There are still a few old shepherds left roaming the hills of Wales, on horseback, accompanied by alert working dogs. Many years ago one of these old shepherds made his way down off the hill, as he often did, to his local watering hole. A journey on horseback, that he took at least once a week and of course the dogs went along and sat obediently around his favorite barstool, which, as anyone who knew him, would immediately vacate out of deferential respect, as he entered the establishment.

One evening he had just drank down half of his favourite pint when a designer dressed tourist, an English man, wandered into the bar remarking, as if leading a major inspection, of the taverns antiquated quaintness.

After assessing this previously, un-encountered environment, with expansive gesticulations, his eyes settled on the shepherd's glass. It was now his opportunity to show everyone that he had knowledge, and wisdom. "I say, would you say, my good man, that your glass is half empty or half full?"

The shepherd dressed in a 1940's woolen three piece suit, that had gained much lanolin from its frequent contact with sheep, looked the man up and down and then glanced at his glass of beer, half of which he had consumed, and replied. "Half empty."

The English man, who had at this time purchased his own pint of exquisite Welsh Ale, was in all fairness, playing his part in satisfying the tourist quota for the area's economic welfare, replied in his polite congenial manner. "Aah, so you are a pessimist?"

The shepherd straightened himself on his barstool and looked the man up and down again before responding. "No, boy bach, I am a Welshman, raised on these bald hills of Wales." His arm pointing through the window at a distant hill under a darkening sky.

The English man displayed a look of apology. "Oh, no sir, what I meant was half empty rather than half full. I suppose when all is said and done it doesn't really matter. Half full or half empty, I suppose there is no real difference."

The shepherd had taken a most definite notice of this man's observation. "Difference, let me tell you, bach, all is not said and done yet, there is a major difference."

"Oh. So you think, perhaps there is a difference?"

"Oh, indeed, bach, a big difference, indeed."

"Please explain."

The shepherd pointed to his glass and picked it up. "This glass is half empty, and now, when I drink the rest of the beer it becomes empty." The shepherd poured down the half and placed the now empty glass on the bar. "Now, if I take your glass of beer", which was still full, "and pour half into my empty glass, it is plain to see that your glass is half empty and my glass is half full."

The Englishman contemplated the explanation and the visual demonstration and spoke. "Do you realize, you have resolved one of life's major philosophical questions. A question that has bothered mankind for millennia?"

"Well, indeed, I will tell you now, that I may have resolved a philosophical problem, but it doesn't help me manage dogs that don't always mind."

He called to one of the dogs back that had strayed. It slinked back to the bar stool, one ear pricked, and one ear flat, acknowledging his masters command with an all knowing, silver eye.

The Englishman was delighted with his new found knowledge. "Well, I have to say, that I have been very impressed with your observations, so please allow me to buy you a drink."

The drink was purchased and the Englishman, after finishing his half empty glass, left to continue his touristic adventures. The shepherd drank down the half of the beer that he had poured into his glass and then with a positive look, contemplated the pint that had just been purchased for him by the generous English tourist.

The landlord smiled at the happy shepherd. "By damned, boy, that is another pint you have gained from your shepherding philosophies."

The shepherd grinned revealing the gaps between his few remaining teeth. "Indeed, that is what you get when you are an optimist."

THE GATHERING

It was a river of sheep moving off the hill.
A bleating mass flowing down a gully to the valley far below.
Wind twisted hawthorns and bracken in the distance were stitching up the moor.
A moving mass of woolen white driven by the collies.
Moorland grass was underfoot with sphagnum moss its base.
Hundreds of years, with little change, a haggard man on pony.
The machine of agriculture has gone ahead but not the hill land shepherd.
Yes, farming sheep has altered little in an ultra modern world.
The shepherd has an electric home and a pretty modern car.
But, to work his living on the open moor it's as if he had a hovel.

THE WELSH SHEPHERD

Where was the Welshman at the beginning of our time?
When our planet was new from its violent heated birth.

He watched the forming of the lands not happy with the seas.
We need great oceans for our ships, for Whales and many fish.

He took a pick and shovel and dug himself a hole.
What he dug out was piled up high and solidified to rock.

People stared in wonder at the Himalayas, the rocky height he'd built.
Water filled the hole he'd dug and they called it the Pacific.

Happy with the work he'd done he gave it to us all.
He returned to Wales with a dog and stick and lived among the sheep.

The finest shepherd he became as he wandered through the clouds.
Every bush and bent of grass, he knew them all quite well.

So when you see the highest rocks and the widest deepest sea.
Remember that old shepherd and his work among our hills.

A TUG OF WAR

The first true Irish pub in the Twin Cities was on the south east corner of Grand and Avon in St Paul, and it was called McCafferty's named for its owner, Ray McCafferty. It was home away from home for many of us from the Isles. They had the familiar Irish and British menu items as well as Guinness Stout and other British style ales. Most evenings had imported live entertainment.

Being the only such gathering place for the self exiled individuals of all classes, educational and career differences did not apply. Labourers, lawyers, truck drivers, doctors, mechanics, architects and many other professions could be found elbow to elbow with each other at the bar all in the congenial, convivial commonality of similar cultural backgrounds.

It was in this environment that a few of us got together and formed a Tug of War team that we would take on the road to area competitions.

Stand up Tug of War was a more recent sporting activity in the Mid West. Previous competitions were all day affairs where those who were pulling had to dig pits that were almost two feet deep. Each puller settled down into his pit and held onto the rope. There didn't seem to be any progress in any direction, and when one puller got tired the pulling would stop and a new puller would take his place.

Stand up Tug of War was the way to go and Pat a man from County Mayo became our coach, and twice a week we practiced in Linwood Park, a short distance from the pub. Every two weeks or so in the summer months we trekked off to a County Fair, sometimes traveling over a hundred miles to compete. We became very good and gained quite a reputation. Of course, the incentive was hard to beat. Ray, the owner, had promised us a free keg of beer for every competition we won, evidenced by the trophies we returned with.

One Saturday we trekked off to Pine City, Minnesota where the Irish National Team was giving a demonstration, and advice to area coaches. There was a competition that day for area teams and for some reason only four of our team showed up. We thought we were out until we realized that only four had shown up from a team that was representing a pub called Moby Dicks, in Minneapolis. The team was an all black team and had little knowledge or training in the art of Tug of War. The four large men were there for the fun of the thing and gladly joined our team and we provided them with McCafferty T-shirts.

We won the competition and invited our new members back to the pub to help us consume the keg of beer. This embarked us on a reciprocal relationship with Moby Dicks, that lasted until McCafferty's closed in the early 1980's.

We had a pleasant following of young ladies and it wasn't long before they were formed up into quite an effective ladies team. One evening at practice we were challenged by the ladies, not to a Tug of War competition but, to a leg wrestling competition. This is where two opponents lie on their backs facing each other side by side with their bottoms barely touching. The idea is to pin you opponent's leg to the ground. Two of the girls demonstrated how it was done.

When one thinks of a male dominated sport like Tug of War it is hard to imagine 'pretty, elegant and feminine', in all its perfections, taking part. However, many of these girls were beauties and belonged to college athletic clubs. It was one of these extraordinary beauties that challenged all the men in turn.

Pat the coach was up for this and got down to take up the challenge. He was faced with a perfectly tanned, sculpted, feminine leg. The main rule is to wave the two inside legs past one another before attempting contact. This done contact was made and in less than two seconds Pat's leg had been pinned. The expression on his face indicated that this was totally unexpected.

It was my turn next and I was defeated in a second and so were all the male team members and some of these were large, strong, athletic men.

We were astonished at how quickly we were all dispatched until one of the other ladies announced that we should not feel too bad about our defeat as our foe was only North America's, Ladies, Leg Wrestling champion.

Although, we enjoyed formal competition we were not opposed to getting involved in pulls where the rules of the game were somewhat limited or should I say unlimited.

One of these competitions took place at the sports facility and picnic area in St Paul's Highland Park. The competition worked by weight not number of feet on the ground. So sometimes we would have nine pulling or eight and occasionally seven. We pulled one team that was made up of twenty young teenagers. To win the competition the winning team had to pull the losing team through a two foot deep pond of very muddy water.

Pat who was in the US Naval, National Guard had to spend the afternoon serving his new country so I was designated as coach for the day. His specific instructions were that when he returned he didn't want to see any member of the team wearing muddy water.

We pulled twenty teams that afternoon and pulled them all through the pond. We were presented with a trophy that was taller than I am. I was hoisted shoulder high by the team members, and I hoisted the trophy even higher. Muddy people everywhere were cheering and applauding. One of the team members asked to handle the trophy so I passed it down to him. A big mistake, because it was then that the rest of the team threw me into the pond.

I scrambled out to much laughter and one of the team shouted out. "You're a great coach, Dingley, we love you."

I joined the laughter. "Well, you have a bloody funny way of showing it."

It was at that moment Pat showed up, looking immaculate in his naval uniform and the first thing out of his mouth was. "Jasus, Dingley, didn't you listen to anything I told you."

Needless to say we had gained another keg of beer.

Our practices in Linwood Park were always fun. We had all kinds of ingenious ways to strengthen our ability and technique. One of which was to sling a rope over a branch about twenty feet up on a large tree and secure it. We would take it in turns to climb the rope with just our hands and once we had achieved the top the coach would have us complete a specified number of pull ups before allowing us to climb back down.

Often on our training forays into the park we were accompanied by an older African American who had a bit of a limp. His name was Vic and somewhere in his background was an Irish ancestor. This is not at all unusual; possibly upwards of eighty percent of African Americans have European blood somewhere in their ancestry.

Vic was a lot of fun and had a great sense of humor and loved to come out and hand out water and towels to the team members as we trained. On one occasion we arrived in the park and the lads were in the process of throwing the rope up over the branch. Across the park was a police car that contained one of St Paul's finest who was watching our activities with great interest because, Vic had seen him when we arrived and had immediately placed his hands behind his back.

The policeman began to drive slowly around the park and Vic spoke to Pat. "Take a look at that cop. I think this could be very interesting."

Pat grinned as the policeman pulled up opposite our little group. Vic had a very sad expression on his face and kept his head hung low, his hands still behind him.

The policeman lowered the window of his air conditioned car and took in the scene counting the individuals involved. The lads were securing the rope and the policeman could contain himself no longer. "So what's going on here, guys?"

Pat leaned into the policeman's face and spoke in a determined angry voice. "We're going to hang him."

I had never seen the colour drain from a face so fast in my life before. He went from a rosy pink to snow white. It lasted a little less than thirty seconds when Vic could not stay serious any longer. He cracked up and laughing, spoke to the policeman. "That scared you didn't it."

"Yes, it did." He continued to look over what we were up to. "So, what are you doing?"

We explained and he stayed around for awhile and watched. He was impressed, so much so, that later, he joined the team.

WILLIAM PEARSON

William Pearson, how he died, I do not know.
The date of his death, March twelve 1884 near Valmont, Colorado.

How he lived and how he talked, I do not know.
I held his handsome jaw bone in my hands.

A miner or a man of note, I do not know.
On a small red rock his name was crudely carved.

What he wore and how he ate, I do not know.
One shining molar remained in the whitened bone.

His deaths ceremony and burial, I do not know.
Without ceremony a Prairie Dog had disinterred him.

Was he close to his world and friends, I do not know.
I laid his remaining bone against his small red rock.

Earth to earth and ashes to ashes, I do not know.
The world of nature has claimed Bill Pearson, forever.

LITTLE BIGHORN

Sitting Bull the master, Crazy Horse his man,
Living way outnumbered on a trail of treaties torn.
Their people had been persecuted from the east into the west.
Now it would continue so they would make a stand.

Yellow Hair's private band mounted on white horses.
The tools of music glinting through the summer leaves.
The journey not for pleasure, but for a people to destroy,
Dirtying an Irish tune throughout those sacred hills.

An easy slaughter for his men, the savage must be gone.
Attack them in their tepees before their day's begun.
Native pride had gathered all to fight the mounted blues.
Surrounding them on higher ground to slaughter 'the one' and all.

The Far West lay at anchor to take the victor home.
His body struck with arrows, the bed on board lay bare.
Punished for transgressions he was slain on greasy grass.
The Morning Star is now at peace, its cruel demon gone.

Custer had intended to fight the Indians, defeat them and then board the Far West, a paddle wheeler that was anchored in readiness on the Upper Little Bighorn River. By all accounts he intended to get back to Washington in time for the centennial celebrations and a possible announcement for a run at the US Presidency.

On his marches he was often accompanied by a brass band, mounted on white horses that often played his favorite tune "The Gary Owen".

He was called the "Son of the Morning Star" by the Indians, because of his early morning attacks on Indian villages.

SHOOT UP AT THE OK CANTEEN

A clay filled gravity dam blocks the upper Towy River, the largest of its kind in the world and Britain's tallest. People from every corner of the British Isles laboured night and day to gain its final height of just over 300 feet. That little upland valley had never seen so many people in the hundreds of years that had passed before, combined. They were only outnumbered by the sheep that peacefully grazed the surrounding hills.

Clay was extracted in the upper moorland reaches and hauled by truck to the site. Rock was quarried and crushed on site and trucks of every shape and size were used to move it into place. In the bottom of the valley, where the water would soon flood, was the nerve center of the operation. This nerve center included a large canteen where continual shifts of workers could sit and eat the food served out through a hatch from an adjoined, extensive kitchen.

A proud, deep voiced, South Walian man by the name of Eddie was in charge. Eddie was being a naughty man. His lovely wife had discovered that he had been having an affair lower down the river in the town of Llandovery, and the lovely wife was angry.

One bright day, while Eddie was busy in the kitchen, the offended, lovely wife came through the front door of the canteen carrying a loaded shotgun. The diners that were munchingly seated either side of the aisle that ran down the middle of the entire building, casually turned to see this female Earp begin her march toward the kitchen.

In a shrill, hag like, voice she called out. "Eddie, where are you, Eddie?" She continued her determined, confident walk and called out again. "Eddie, where are you? I want to see you, Eddie"

Eddie's head appeared through the hatch and his deep baritone voice rang out through the whole building. "Here I am my love, here I am."

She immediately raised the large weapon to her shoulder and pulled one of the triggers under its double barrel. She had never fired a shotgun before, and the recoil almost landed her on her backside. The gun discharged its leaded content into the ceiling of the building splintering wood off the joists which held up the roof.

Diners were clambering over each other to gain cover under the tables. Eddie too had gone for protection no doubt beginning to realize the folly of his recent ways.

Two brave men tackled the woman. It was an international effort one that would have made the United Nations proud. One Welshman and one Irishman, the Irishman gripped the gun and the Welshman helped to part her from it. The gun was cracked open and the discharged cartridge was discarded. The unfired cartridge was removed and the Irishman handed it to the woman. "Ah, now, my darlin' you's'd be better off if you threw it at him and it would be safer for the rest of us."

Eddie had crept back to the serving hatch and gingerly peered through. The international collaboration held the gun and let the angry, wronged woman proceed to finish her mission.

She took two steps toward the wayward husband and threw the leaden cartridge. It was far more accurate than the one that had been discharged through the barrel of the gun. Eddie had to duck and it whistled past his head. He kept his eye on the scorned and angry wife who was reminding him of his marriage vows as the cartridge hit a plate on a tall shelf in the kitchen. This plate, the first of dozens, crashed into its neighbor and began a china breaking, domino cascade that went on for almost a minute. Eddie was in the midst of these clattering shards as they deepened around his feet, he would be responsible for their replacement.

He shuffled his feet as if to try and avoid breaking the china into smaller shards. His lovely, angry wife glared at him and there was no doubt that he would no longer continue his extra marital adventures. The broken china reminding him how close his life had come to being completely shattered.

GOOD OLD ABE

Abram the butcher. Had the better shop in town.
The best of beef, the finest lamb and the bacon close to home.
A foot of counter in his shop was worth a land of many fields.
The meat across that counter small fed all from town and farm.
He worked his life from skin to bone and laid out joints and chops.
After all was cut and done his years of trade complete,
He sold his shop to wander as his mind began to fail

Today he walks the town with little in his head.
The shop from brain and high street is gone these many years.
His former customers he sees and doesn't know a one.
He finds his way around the streets with the remnants of his soul.
His thoughts come quick and barely form in a brain that's full of holes.
He sees a glimpse of something past but it's gone before he knows,
And all the wanderings through the town will never find these thoughts.

They greet him on the street where his butcher's life was made.
The respect he earned throughout his life is a prize he knows no more.
The town is his and he knows not why because yesterday is gone.
His feet may know the streets and their pavements either side.
Those streets could be in any town for his foot has left his heart.
On his way he loses track but is happy on the trail
For a former friend or neighbor will guide him back to home.

A MAN OF ROCK

His was a life of splintered rock,
Dressed for shape and chiseled sleek.
Quarry hewn and rubble picked.
Sinewed muscle pitching off to fit,
Not a statue's stone cold flesh.

Heaving granite to his banker's bench,
Exploring shape to seek within.
Creating rubble when hewn to size.
Beautied, tracered from broad rough hands.
Keystone, lintel, plinth and a ready, pretty sill.

How long will the great walls stand?
A quarried mouth in a mountain side?
He has given us a wordless statement of the past,
Shaped and placed to mark the lands.
It's a rubbled life without his strength.

A banker is the name given to a stone dressing bench. Stone is worked with a variety of chisels, three of the major ones being a pitcher, a point and a tracer.

MY SURGERY

I think about the knife again and the cutting of my flesh.
"Let's cut it out and save a life from an agonizing death."
Do the cuts of life keep a knifes edge to bring an end so clean?
How often is it blunted as we stumble through the years?
No finer edge in our youthful eyes on the day we first can love.
When the heart is broken do we hone to make it cut again?
Let's hope we can and not give in before we have our slice.
Those are the bladed days that fill the weeks of carving out our work.
While gathering up our croppings to keep our basket full.
Cutting out our living to feed our pulsing heart.
Sabering out existence as we run it through our days.
Cleaving through the seasons where we delineate our years.

A COOK WITH ROMANTIC INTENT

Sunday evenings at the Irish Well were mostly devoid of customers except for an Irish Music Seisiun which began at about nine thirty in the evening. These seisiuns were some of the best in the Twin Cities and often featured some of the world's finest Irish talent. Up to thirty musicians would show up playing fiddles, squeeze boxes, concertinas, banjos, guitars, bouzoukis, whistles, flutes, uilleann pipes, and with their periphery often crowded by a whole cadre of bodhran playing, Irish Music wannabe's.

On one particular Sunday the world's finest had indeed come together for one of the best seisiuns ever, even if you included all those that took place in Ireland. It was on this evening that a wayward trucker happened to drop in for a quick beer and a bowl of Irish Stew, which was the only food available on Sundays. On his feet were cowboy boots that went with his jeans and western shirt. However the western look stopped at his neck. On his head he had a grubby, greasy baseball cap that had the name of his employer embroidered on the front. Poking out from under this, rarely removed cap, were great bunches of equally greasy hair. He stared at the large group of musicians that included seven fiddlers, all playing in unison. He pointed to them. "What is this s***?"

I replied, realizing that he probably wouldn't know what an Irish Music Seisiun was. "That is the Irish Well Orchestra."

His eyes widened. "No s***. You have an orchestra in this bar?"

I smiled. "Indeed we do, there they are."

The stew was served and every spoonful was sandwiched between intense stares that were doing their best to keep up with the intense Celtic lilt emanating throughout the room.

He finished his meal, drank down what remained of his beer, paid the bill and left to continue his journey. I was certain that in all the places he would stop on his highwayed excursions across the US, they would hear about that bar in St Paul Minnesota, that had its own orchestra.

On Wednesday evenings there was another regular group that came in to talk and philosophize about how to solve the problems of the world. They called themselves the Celtic Mensa group and several other customers were quite fond of pointing out, that surely, Celtic Mensa was an oxymoron. I soon began to call the evening the night of the high IQs.

One evening I was approached by one of their number, a very polite well meaning woman. Her name was Vera, she was over six feet tall and carried a figure that made ample seem like skinny. She indicated that she was a leading expert in one of those eastern methods of food preparation. I had never heard of it before and I knew that it was about as far from bangers and mash, and Irish stew, as you could get.

She asked how much I would charge if I allowed her to use the pub's kitchen on Sundays to prepare this, full of 'eastern promise' cuisine, which she would serve to the dedicated followers of her dietary adventures. I told her there would be no charge if she paid for the food and staff required to serve as long as I was allowed to sell alcohol to her guests. A time was agreed that would have them finish up as the Irish Music Seisiun started so the diners could move from 'eastern promise' onto Irish promise.

The first of these evenings went very well, as would the others. Vera had her helpers clean the kitchen following each event and that was a bonus and a great example to the cooks and staff that worked there the rest of the week. At the end of the evening and before the Seisiun started I patted Vera on her back and thanked her. She had brought forty people in and I had sold some drinks.

After the first couple of weeks the business increased and Vera too was a more frequent visitor to the pub and began taking an interest in the other events. I didn't realize it at the time but it seemed that Vera was taking my positive congratulatory comments on her efforts as romantic overtures.

She began to take part in the open-mic evenings. At first it was a poem and on other occasions she would play guitar and sing a romantic verse or two. Later to the surprise of, myself, my staff, and the audience she would read segments each week out of a sex manual. Although it was an uncensored open-mic the audiences were taken by surprise. It wasn't that they were shocked, after all they were a mature audience, and just about all of them had heard it all before. I asked one of my staff about it and the reply shocked me. "She is doing this for your benefit. You do know that she is in love with you, don't you?"

I didn't know. I now realized that I was the most innocent, naïve person in that den of worldly bohemians. "Why is she in love with me?" I asked. "Why can't she pick on someone her own size?"

"Don't ask me. You must have encouraged her. She talks about you all the time."

"Encourage her, the only encouragement I have given her, is make positive comments about her work here."

"See, that's what happens."

I wanted to do something about it, but I couldn't decide what. I went on as usual with the exception of delivering my positive comments from some distance away from her. She continued to read from the sex manual and after one reading she had asked one of my staff if I knew that she liked orgasms. It soon became the inside story that people would hear vague snippets of, and actually make special trips to the pub to find out what the latest was.

One open-mic evening I was in the kitchen cutting up a sheep carcass for the coming weeks batch of Irish stew when one of my staff informed me that Vera had taken the stage and was about to read the latest installment from the sex manual.

The kitchen was behind the backstage wall and the doors into and out of the kitchen were on either side. So it was easy to creep up to and stand in the door way, and hear what was going on, on stage, without being seen.

I listened as Vera began to describe the sex act. "And the man takes his penis and inserts it into the woman's vagina just half an inch to tease her."

This was my chance. This was my opportunity to finish this once and for all. I burst through the door and placed myself at the foot of the stage and announced as loudly as I could. "Bloody hell, woman, what do you mean, tease the woman with half an inch. Some of us poor men, a half inch is all we have." The crowd roared and I returned to my cleaver.

Unfortunately, it had made no impression on her and later that week while lying in bed in the early morning, resting after a heavy work night at the pub, I heard a guitar being played outside my window and a woman's voice, softly singing.

I moved slowly in the bed so that I could position myself to peek through the blinds, without moving them or being heard, or seen, from the outside. There was Vera on the lawn outside my window. She had laid out a decorative blanket with wild flowers strewn around the edges and others were around her head. She was sitting in the middle of the blanket playing her guitar and singing love songs. I was reminded of what it must have been like to witness the hippie activities at Woodstock back in the sixties. She must have decided that if the sex manual approach didn't work then it would have to be music and flower power.

I was trapped in my apartment. I lay there very still, afraid to move, in case she realized that I was in residence. An hour and a half later she gave up on her determined effort to woo me and left the scene. Needless to say I had a late breakfast that morning.

My sister and her daughter flew over for a visit and soon found that the Irish Well was a little different to the pubs in Builth Wells. However, they were enjoying the eclectic events that occurred there. I mentioned the Vera problem and was surprised to learn that they had been well informed by the locals. I pointed out that I wasn't sure what to do about it and it was then I was told that my staff had been winding her up.

So the following Monday morning I called a meeting of all my staff, all twenty of them. I smiled at each one in turn nodding my head to acknowledge. It was rare that I had them all in one place at the same time. "Alright, you lot." I began, "I hear you have been winding up Vera as to my romantic aspirations for her. I can tell you now, unequivocally, I have no romantic inclinations for that woman, whatsoever. So I am charging you with the task of unwinding her so that my life can get back to normal. What you say and what you do is up to you, but get her off my back is all I ask of you."

The last sentence I said was probably a big mistake, however it worked. A week or so later I met Vera coming across the street and she was upset and well into a blubbering state of affairs. "What's up with you?" I asked.

"They told me that you are promiscuous."

I had not expected this, however I seized on the opportunity to finish this thing once and for all. "Vera, if you had asked me when we first met, I could have told you that."

That did it. Within the week the 'eastern promise' meals came to an end and she had left the area. It was a shame, because I had not wanted to hurt her in any way. She might have had a high IQ, however, when it came down to reading the behavioral signs of her fellow human beings she didn't seem to have a clue. It was as if she were stuck in her early teen years. However, her activities will remain quite vivid in the memories of those who witnessed them. I hope she has learned since and got over her time providing 'eastern promise' to the world of the Celt.

THE RIGHTS OF ALL OF US

His red hair moved with every step a grin upon his face.
The parchment in his hand was ready for his pen.
A declaration in his head would say it for the land.
He gathered up the thoughts of those who knew the task ahead,
The documents of freedom and the rights of every man.

A nation would be founded on that parchments trail of ink.
Freedom from the tyrants no longer to be served.
A voice from all the people would, now, rule the land.
Religion will be parted from the running of the state
And happiness pursued without the fear of hate.

The power of this parchment has lasted many years.
Self evidence of truth has struggled to stay free.
The equality of man has been challenged many times,
The testing's of a nation that such would long endure,
That for and of and by the people shall never let us down.

Today we have a president that is letting down the guard,
Perpetrating tyranny and trampling on the rights.
There is little for the people who die in foreign lands
While those few, no longer equal, are gathering in the wealth.
He has wedged a god between the state and justice once for all.

This man knows nothing of the parchments that set a nation straight,
The principles of freedom to be defended every day,
The rights of individuals to pursue their happy way.
He will never do abroad what he will not do at home
For only rights upheld will flower in the world.

This world now sees hypocrisy where once was USA.
There is a fear in many countries that he will stay for many years.

The hope for all our futures is a vote from many hands.
May the gods stay in the church so the state may rule for all
To separate this man from a planet losing hope.

    The preceding was written after listening to the comments on the US President, in 2004, from friends in other countries. Their comments were often sharper than the comments from the US critics.

GUNNED DOWN IN MY STREET

He had been accused of stealing a cell phone.
When he left the building an ambush was called in.
In half a block a rain of bullets hit him to the bone
And then another, the night air shattered by the din.

He was dead, but it didn't stop the gunman's crime,
The automatic weapon was fired through the chest.
Bloody revenge was carried out, many bullets at a time.
They made a hole down in the street where they came to rest.

He was only twenty one, his life was just beginning.
The cell phone was not stolen and was later found.
Lost by the murderer down his sofa, if only it was ringing.
I know all this, because that boy was killed ten feet from my ground.

A NOT SO NICE SET OF CUSTOMERS

The Irish Well was a sociologists dream. Just about every aspect of the human condition could be found there and none more offensive than a group of white Southern, US, pipe fitters who were in the northern state of Minnesota for a major pipe fitting job. They had become residents of the Motel that surrounded the pub itself.

For the first few days of their stay they seemed to be reasonably well behaved even though they were a little crude around the edges. After a week or so they began to behave in a way that indicated that the pub was theirs and they were in control. Big trouble it seemed was just around the corner and on a weekend night when the place was full for the food and entertainment I was called over to a large booth where six of these southern men had made themselves at home.

I smiled. "Yes, gentlemen, how can I help you?"

The response was a horrifying revelation. "John, we like your bar, but we have a problem, John, a big problem and you have to take care of it for us."

"I am sorry to hear that. I will do what I can. What is the problem?"

"John, you have niggas in this bar and we don't like niggas. They offends us. We is white gentlemen from the south and they should know better than to be in a place where white folks is. We want you to get them outta here."

I looked at them with a stunned stare and it seemed like an age before I could respond. The Irish Well like most of the other establishments in the area welcomed everyone no matter what their colour or culture. My staff were a cross section of color, ethnic and cultural backgrounds. I eventually spoke and I was not very happy with this situation and knew that there was going to be more trouble than I could possibly handle.

I allowed myself to become irate, it was the only way I could muster up the strength to deal with the situation. "Let me tell you something. We don't care what color our customers are and those black gentlemen

45

that are here are valued customers and number among our regulars. If you don't like this situation then this place is not for you and I think you should be the ones to move yourselves along. Your kind we can do without."

They rose to their feet as one. It seemed that I had grossly offended their bigoted sensibilities and I was referred to as a Yankee Son of a B****. Several patrons also rose to their feet and came forward to back me up, if that sort of help was going to be needed. I felt it would be, because I had an overwhelming feeling that my time on this planet had become severely limited. I followed these southern white bigots down the hallway to the door where just outside, to my surprise and pleasure, three St Paul police cars were waiting. The police began grabbing them as they left the building and placed them in handcuffs.

As the last one was going through the door he turned and threw a fist into my face. I moved back slightly and the blow hit me square in the mouth. I fell back and was caught by one of the magnificent posse that had risen to support me.

The police had grabbed the offender and I pulled my fist back, which was blooded from my mouth, to return the blow that I had received. His arms were pinned back by the officer, who was placing him in handcuffs, and I have to admit, fair play was very far from my thoughts. I just wanted to belt him one. However, before I could, the policeman warned me that I would be arrested also. I stopped, disappointed.

The miscreant bigots were never seen again, I believe they were escorted to the state line and threatened never to return. It seemed that they had been causing trouble all over town.

This, of course was not the last of them. There were two left. One was a brute of a man called, Big John, about six feet seven inches tall, and the other was also quite tall, about six feet two inches. Although, he didn't look that big when he stood beside his larger friend.

It was a Friday evening and the very popular Irish entertainer, Peter Yates was in town to play on the Irish Well Stage. I had spent the early evening making preparations for a busy night and had taken a break to take a rest, when I returned the place was packed and the music was in full swing.

As I came down the passage into the pub I was confronted by one of the female wait staff, who to say the least was quite upset. "You have to do something about that man at the bar."

"What man?"

She pointed out Big John who, it seemed, was sitting quite peacefully at the topside of the bar where there were chairs rather than barstools. His friend was sitting next to him and seemed a little worse for wear and his head was nodding like a bobble head dog that you sometimes see in the back windows of cars.

As she pointed she informed me that he was offering, in a crude manner, one hundred dollar bills for a blow job.

I pointed out that it was a drink, and she immediately responded that it was not a drink he was after, and that I should do something about it right away.

I said I would deal with it, and before I could get to him I was approached by another of the female wait staff who had the same complaint.

The man and his bobbling headed friend were sitting in the two chairs closest to the back door. I looked down at Big John and tapped him on the shoulder. He looked up, I smiled. "Hi, Big John, I understand that you have been offering money to my staff for a blow job."

"Yea, the goddamned b*****'s."

I stayed calm. "Now, Big John, I am sure you can get what you are looking for in this town, somewhere, but you won't find it here. So I would rather you didn't harass my staff."

He picked up a handful of change and threw it into the bar where it clinked and clattered against the bottles. "Godamn you, you Yankee Son of a B****."

Here we go again, I thought. I turned and went around the bar through the kitchen door to get behind the bar to talk to the bartender, and have him not serve them anymore, and then perhaps they would leave without trouble. I met the bartender in the kitchen. I was surprised, because there were tears rolling down his cheeks. "What's the matter with you?" I asked.

Oh," he said, "that man at the bar said he is going to get his gun and come back here and shoot me, and I don't know what to do."

"What man?"

We moved to where we could see the people who were sitting around the bar and he pointed to Big John. "That's him. He means it, he is going to come back and shoot me."

I was absolutely furious and I told my stressed bartender that as soon as I could get the man on his feet he was to call the police.

I walked back into the bar. The whole place was flooded with the happy, Irish Music and the whisky voice of Peter Yates. I marched up to Big John, and this time I was livid and at the top of my voice I screamed. "Get on your feet, you great big bullying monster and go and get your gun. You come in here threatening to shoot my staff, well you go and get your gun and come back and shoot me you worthless piece of humanity."

He stared up at me from his chair and slowly he lifted himself out of it. He got taller, and taller, and taller. His head and shoulders rose up past mine and he was still getting taller, and taller. I became terrified. What was I getting myself into? He stared down at me. An angrier man I had rarely seen. I noticed his hands, they were bigger than large bladed shovels. Those hands could have torn me apart in seconds and any response I might have been able to muster would have been grossly futile. I was ready to give it all up and run for my life.

The music had stopped and there was a pin drop silence throughout the bar. Just when I thought the moment of my demise had come the back door opened and a former cook came in and reached up and placed his hand on Big John's shoulder from behind. "Hey, Big John, someone wants to see you outside."

The big man turned slightly and I seized the opportunity and spoke again. "Go and see who it is. It's probably a blow job waiting for you."

I didn't think he would, but he made for the door. "Take your friend with you." I added.

He reached out his right arm and took his friend by the scruff of his neck and lifted him straight up out of his seat as if he were a frail rag doll. As they went through the door they were grabbed by three police officers and quickly handcuffed. I turned to the bartender who was busy dialing the phone. "Don't bother, they've got him."

The phone was hung up and the back door was closed. The place was still in total silence, and I was still trembling with fear, when there was a loud strum on the large acoustic guitar, that Peter played. Then he spoke in his rich, Irish Whiskey voice. "Ladies and gentlemen I would now like to dedicate my next tune to the heavy weight champion of Wales, John Dingley."

There was a huge roar from the crowd and happiness was restored.

THE OLD OAK

That acorn when it sprouted, was it in the parking lot?
Perhaps surrounded by a meadow and pretty flowers in spring.
It grew its many branches giving shade on sunny days.
Then ugly buildings encroached around its handsome trunk.

Pretty meadows disappeared when the concrete was laid down.
The rain now dripping from the leaves never finding soil
Splashing on the black top to run into a drain.
But that tree stood fast and blossomed every year.

The cars that parked around it were shielded from the sun.
The greed for space spelled doom for that old oak.
No one cared to save it with its branches full of leaves
It was chain-sawed and removed to park ONE shiny car.

They call it being practical taking nature from our eyes.
How can a large brain defy that which gave it birth?
Nature soon will strike us back to take us from the scene.
Because it is not perfect; we are its big mistake.

A BOG IN ST PAUL

An old limestone retaining wall between two houses in St Paul, Minnesota was falling apart, crumbling away from the onslaughts of winter and organic acids. It had to be taken down and replaced with a wall of pleasant appearance, and structural integrity. The numbers were turned in and the job was mine.

The wall belonged to a very fussy, mathematical type of human being who knew nothing of wall demolition or wall construction. However, he insisted in critiquing every aspect of the work, even of things that were of no importance, whatsoever. The old wall, made of a Platteville Limestone had deteriorated considerably, and had to be removed completely, and a new footing dug. It wasn't a tall wall. It topped out at two foot six and was about eighty feet long.

All the work had to be done from the neighbor's property as the wall was only three feet from its owner's house. Permission was asked for and given by a pleasant neighbor, an individual called Jim, who was a recently retired St Paul policeman. He had one condition, and that was, could we remove his old, cracked and unlevel, concrete patio. This was agreed.

My friend Ray and his Bobcat were called in to demolish and remove the wall, and in addition, the old patio. Ray was one of those Bobcat driving experts, where it always seemed that when he climbed aboard the thing it was as if he were putting on a comfortable overcoat. Ray and the machine would become one.

Jim had indicated that the concrete had no iron reinforcing rods so could be easily broken up for removal. And he had decided to leave for his cabin, somewhere on a lake in the north woods and gave me a phone number where he could be reached if any problems came along while working on his property. There were no utilities to avoid and Ray unloaded the Bobcat.

David, a hard working dairy sheep farmer, from Wisconsin, had come along to help me for a couple of days and we all got down to work.

The first part of the wall came out easily and David and I began hand digging the footing as it was close to the house while Ray began his work to remove the old patio, which was right up to the wall of Jim's house. After a minute or two we could see that the concrete was not breaking up like it was supposed to. There may not have been reinforcing rods; however there were all sorts of metal objects, including an iron bedstead, which had been used instead. Ray managed to slide the whole thing away from the house, and then after a considerable amount of time and effort he was able to break it up and dump it into his truck.

With the patio out of the way Ray could get to the rest of the wall. It was not to be, as soon as the Bobcat began crossing the area where the patio had been it began to sink, quite rapidly.

Ray bailed out and came over to me and David, and announced, in an alarmed voice. "John, the Bobcat is sinking."

Indeed it was. We stood there open mouthed as the muddy, watery ooze covered the bucket and the front wheels and was about to cover the rear wheels when it slowly stopped.

Ray was on the verge of panic. "We've got to get it out of there or we are going to lose it."

We agreed and David suggested that we hook it up with chains to his Ford Bronco, which he would keep out on the street for traction. Ray gingerly climbed back onto the Bobcat and placed it in reverse as David pulled. Fortunately its removal was quite straight forward. However, the bog that we had discovered, that had been oozing under Jim's old patio, was a major barrier to the continuation of the work.

I called Jim and explained the situation; also letting him know, that the patio was reinforced, although not with reinforcing rods. He told me to deal with the bog and give him a bill for the extra work.

Ray carefully approached the bog with the Bobcat and at its edge began to scoop out the dripping, oozing marsh. Two truckloads were eventually dug out amounting to some fourteen cubic yards. The bog's removal left behind a hole that went down to the depth of the basement footing. I called Jim and recommended that if he wanted to install a new patio the hole should be filled with gravel. He asked me to go ahead and that he would be returning the next day.

Fourteen cubic yards of gravel were hauled in and compacted into that hole and it was only then that Ray could get to remove the rest of the old wall.

The new wall's construction proceeded with no further surprise events. Jim returned and I presented him with the bill for the gravel, there was no charge for the extra work as he had allowed us to use his property to get to the wall.

When Jim saw the bill, he was upset and muttered a few, not too happy words, and went into the house for a check. After ten minutes or so of waiting I began to wonder if he had slipped away through his back door or had decided to not pay me at all.

After another few minutes he came out of the house carrying a can of beer in each hand, and between two fingers of his right hand was the check, which he pushed toward me. He had a huge smile on his face. "Here's your money and I am happy to pay it. Have a beer, you deserve it."

I was stunned by this turn around and I commented. "You've had a change of mood, haven't you?"

'Yes, I have. I have lived in this house for twenty three years and it's the first time I have had a dry basement."

MY PARISH

What is a Llanafan man?
A Red Lion life of darts and quoits?
Bearing out from the sheep grazed grass,
The livestock news from a market pen.

What is a Llanafan man?
Who lives in rain with feet in mud
And whistles dogs that rarely mind.
With sweat combined with wet from cloud.

What is a Llanafan man?
Who in a rare blue sunshine sky
Harvests grass with determined zeal.
To pack in barns for winters feed.

What is a Llanafan man?
Who knows no other life than his
And asks no question beyond his bounds.
Whose world is full and needs no more.

What is a Llanafan man?
When a Red Lion pint is his reward,
Greeting his like with a social smile
The pub erupts in song, he is better than us all.

THE HAIRCUT

I was raised on a Welsh hill farm surrounded by sheep and the wilds of life that populated an area that was mostly devoid of people. Limited access to the so called civilized world isolated the sparse human population. No modern conveniences, such as electricity and indoor plumbing, were available and transportation was intermittent at best. Neighbors and friends would visit occasionally, usually on horseback, dropping by after visiting the local pub or returning from a shepherding foray into the wild uplands. It was on one of these occasions when Gibb Lewis dropped by on his way to his own isolated hill farm.

Gibb Lewis was not only a hill farmer, he was a talented craftsman. He was renowned for making sturdy baskets including beautifully made whisket baskets, shepherd crooks, and walking sticks.

He would ask young men, when the opportunity arose, "When is the right time to cut a stick, boy?" There would be an assortment of seasonal answers and then he would smile, "When you see it."

As well as baskets and sticks, he made besoms, those wonderful sweeping devices often referred to as witch's brooms. His workmanship would make any flighty witch proud of her transport. His were the Cadillac of sweepers. He was also noted hedger and a master of many other rural crafts. There was always one thing that he wanted people to know, and that was the fact that he was the same age as the year.

I was nine years old at the time of his visit. He was a friendly man who had a distinctive glint in his eye, but even more distinctive was the way he pushed up his lower lip over his upper lip when he was about to speak. This action was a forewarning of a possible exposing of rural wisdom, with words that you could not back away from hanging on to.

After buying one of his exquisitely made baskets my mother asked if he knew anything about cutting hair. The bottom lip pushed up. She was ready for his answer. "Well, Mrs. Dingley, I have learned that skill, because I have done the lords bidding and came forth and multiplied. I have sons and I crop their heads before they are blinded by their hair."

My mother was pleased. "Good, then I wonder if you could cut John's hair before *he* becomes blind."

The lip pushed up again. "Indeed, Mrs. Dingley, the boy should be cropped. Do you have a comb, a scissors and a hair clippers? Of course, I could use a sheep shears, if you have one, and don't have the proper tools."

I hoped he was joking.

Mother soon supplied a comb and scissors and then spent ten minutes scrambling through drawers to find a set of clippers. The clippers she found, to say the least, had clipped in better times. As she handed them to Gibb she said. "They are old, and haven't been used for some time."

"Well, we can hope, Mrs. Dingley, that as we get old we will be used less. The important thing, of course, is can we keep our edge."

I didn't realize, at the time, how prophetic his statement was.

He looked the clippers over. "I will do what I can with them," was his comment as he squeezed the handles in anticipation of the task ahead.

I was seated backwards on a chair and a towel was thrown around my neck and tucked into my shirt collar.

Gibb went to work and at first the hair was combed and snipped with the scissors. So far so good, and then my head was ready for the clippers. Gibb's left hand was clamped to the top of my head eliminating all potential movement. The clippers were clicking slowly up the back of my neck until they pulled and failed to cut two or three of the hairs it was aimed at. It hurt, I squealed. He backed up the clippers pulling out the two or three hairs. I wasn't really counting. I squealed again. Mother admonished me and told me to sit still.

I could feel this, part time, country barber, smiling at my mother. "Don't you worry, Mrs. Dingley, we can tie him down, if we have too." He chuckled, "you might want to have a cord handy."

Mother believed him; however she did not go in search of a cord. Instead, I received another admonition. "You will sit still, if you know what is good for you, John David Dingley."

I did the best I could under the excruciating circumstances.

Every attempt that Gibb made would result in a hair or two pulled, and a squeal. Although, mother was continuing to admonish me for my painful outbursts and futile attempts to get away, Gibb in all fairness came to my defense and explained to her that it was the fault of the clippers, and not the tortured boy, with his tear stained cheeks.

The task was completed. My squealing out had, somewhat unnerved Gibb, and I think he was as glad as I was that it was over.

He addressed my mother once more. "Well, I can tell you now, Mrs. Dingley that after all that noise you should have him quiet for quite for some time."

For years following this ordeal whenever I ran into Gibb he would remind me of that stressful day. The lower lip would move up and he would give me an intense look. "Do you remember when I cut your hair, boy?"

"I do Gibb, I do, I remember it well. How could I forget?"

He would continue. "A stuck pig could not have squealed more, but fair play to you, you stuck it out even though those clippers were in need of a good sharpening. I told your mother that it would be very few who could have stuck it out like you did."

I would smile. "I had to stick it out, Gibb, because you had me in a grip that I couldn't get away from."

I still wonder to how many people he told of the story of my torturous ordeal.

THE HEDGER

It was raining again and was splashing on his cap.
He wore it in reverse to shed the water from his neck.
The billhook, too, was wet as it sliced the Hazel wood.
The old border hedge was being laid again.
Like the hair upon his head the bushes straggled wild.
Hazel, Blackthorn, Alder, Willow, Hawthorn and the rest.
Plaited in the branches their growing purpose one.
The entanglement of species barriered together.
The grooming of the wild was this man's intent.
Another pleacher cut and placed precisely through its heart.
Weaving through the stakes and hethering it down.
Keeping neighbors good while separating fields.

A pleacher is a live sapling like stick that is cut three-quarters of the way through at an angle close to the ground. This weakens it enough so that it can be bent over to lie through the hedge.

Hethering, is a basket weaved edge of straight green sticks that ties down and tops off the hedge.

AN EXPLOSIVE COLLISION

In the mid nineteen twenties two old farmer friends met on Builth Wells High Street. The usual pleasantries were exchanged and then the discussion of the prominent local news of the day took place. The first major car accident of the area had occurred two or three days earlier.

"Boy, did you hear about what happened to two of those new fangled, mechanical carriages. They met on the road, you know, and they didn't stop."

"Oh, duw, indeed," responded the other, "I had heard about it. I was told that it was a terrible explosion, the beginning of Armageddon, the end cannot be far behind."

"No, no ,no, boy bach. A collision it was, not an explosion."

"I can't see that there is any difference. It was a terrible thing."

"Difference, difference. Well, there is a tremendous difference between the two."

"I don't see it."

"You, don't see it. Well, I will tell you what the difference is. In a collision there you are. In an explosion, where are you?"

TO BUILD

Dimensional, modular block of baked clay.

Clay, the inorganic dusts of time.

Time, a one way distance to eternity.

Eternity, a place without a finite end.

End, the other side of a starting point.

Point, a precise indication or location without shape.

Shape, specific, measured or free in form.

Form, from the dusts of time and a ready mold.

Mold, a modular frame for a block dimensional.

It's amazing what can be done with a brick.

DECORAH

Aah, Decorah, a city on the edge of influence.

The capital of a planet of border line indulgence.

Does a person, who makes it here, make it anywhere?

A place where the tribes of culture indulge with unlike friends.

Homogenizing worlds that pioneer the "in crowd" trends.

Are people able to shine in their individual efforts?

Certainly the home of great things no less.

A bluff cycled trail through the land of the driftless.

Are you ready with the world to follow the eagles?

A RESONANT PLACE

I keep returning to the Irish Well and all its myriad adventures. The upstairs kitchen was connected to its ballroom counterpart, directly below by a large concrete stairwell. On happy days, fortunately there were many, preparing for opening and coordination of kitchen staff, I would sing much to my staff's surprise Welsh hymns, folk songs, snippets of opera and a few poorly remembered tunes of the more modern era.

The one thing I noticed was the incredible resonance in the stairwell. Singing there was an astounding, sounding experience. It was if the entire stairwell was singing for you.

One evening there was an event in the ballroom that was being attended by a friend by the name of Roderick Phipps Kettlewell. Rod, a talented musician was classically trained, a concert pianist, a conductor of orchestra, and chorus, and also composed music.

He wanted to join me in the upstairs bar for a drink and I suggested we take the less congested route through the kitchen and up the resonant stairway. I had Rod stop half way up and told him that he was in a place where you could feel music better than in a concert hall. I stepped up the next flight of steps, turned and sang a Welsh folk tune, higher than ever before and managed, because of the resonance, a couple of easy high C's.

His eyes widened and his first comment was, "Wow!" and then, "This must be the Irish Well's best kept secret."

Nothing more was said about this until the Minnesota Opera were holding auditions at the famous Ordway Concert Hall. Rod was chosen to be the accompanist for the auditioning singers. The Ordway, having quite the reputation, was attracting singers from around the world and occasionally Rod would bring back one or two of the participants to the Irish Well for food and cocktails.

On one of these occasions Rod nudged me and whispered. "Take this man," indicating the opera singer, "and let him experience 'the sound'."

I was surprised at the request but took the man along, anyway. In the stairwell I stood and sang for him.

His response was the same as Rod's had been, "Wow!"

I smiled and said, "Your turn."

He refused. "I couldn't do that." He said.

There was no doubt that his professionalism prevented him from doing so and also for him, it was totally unexpected and I think it may have embarrassed him a little. What he said to Rod about the experience I never got to know.

The above scenario would happen several times during the Minnesota Opera Season. The male singers invariably refused to sing, however the sopranos all gave it a try and it was incredibly impressive and a joy for me as some of these singers were well known performers on the Metropolitan Stage.

One warm summer the mixed Sydney, Welsh Chorus, was touring the US and there was a two concert stop in the Twin Cities. Following one of the concerts, the Irish Well hosted a banquet, paid for by the St David's Society of Minnesota. Great singing and conviviality followed in the bar and Rod, who had also attended, encouraged me to take Margaret the chorus director to the stairwell.

Margaret, although coming from Australia was originally from somewhere in the South Wales Valleys. I led her through the kitchen and into the stairwell and sang one verse, in Welsh, of a folk tune.

When I had finished she stared at me with an uncomfortable expression. She seemed to be totally overwhelmed, not by the singing, but by the fact that I had actually subjected her to this, to her mind, strange musical onslaught.

I smiled. "Your turn."

Her eyebrows went up, and her eyes actually widened. "You can bugger off."

As we made our way back through the kitchen to the bar she turned to me and quite forthrightly said. "You're a bloody nutter, you are."

She had captured it. I don't think I could have put it better myself.

THE FACT OF EVOLUTION

"I don't believe in evolution."
She said, with an unflinching air of authority.
A raised eyebrow replied, "Surely it is not a belief?"
"Well, it's just a theory, then, isn't it?"

The eyebrow stayed up, "Do you know what a theory is?"
"It's just what somebody thinks, it's nothing really."
The eyebrow smiled. "A theory comes from a body of evidence.
Gathered from precise observations and the testing of the same.

"No evidence has ever been found that discounts evolution.
If it had, there would not be a theory.
Every testing observation has incontrovertibly proven evolution.
The theory of evolution has never been disproved since 1859.

"To say evolution is a belief is to express scientific ignorance
And your air of authority and confidence will never prove a thing."
Then a shaking head replaced the eyebrow smile.
His words would not make her evolve.

ONE FOR HEAVEN AND ONE FOR HELL

The Red Lion Inn in Llanafan Fawr is said to be the oldest in the county of Powys. Opposite the heavy oak, front door is St Afan's Church and grave yard. Back in the early 1900's as in earlier years religion was said to rule the many minds, and making a living was wrested from a struggle with nature and lots of sheep.

Two men from outside the community were noted rabbit poachers and knew where and when to capture these animals that could be sold on to the English cities for profit. The countryside of Wales was full of rabbits and when an outsider asked some locals how many they thought there might be, the first response was, "A tidy few." His contemporary disagreed. "No, no, boy, there is more than that, they are sniving." The outsider appeared to be no wiser even though every local in the pub knew the preciseness of those answers.

The two poachers, in a few hours, had made a considerable dent in the rabbit population. There was no doubt that their numbers had been reduced from sniving to a tidy few. Each poacher carried on his back a large grain sack stuffed with the paunched corpses. In the dark of the night they struggled with the weight and decided that they would hide their catch over the churchyard wall, where they would eventually share them out.

It was a large effort to get them over the wall and as they did so a couple of rabbits fell out onto the roadside ditch. "Leave them," the one said, "we can get them later. Let's go and have a pint in the pub."

Poaching of course is thirsty work and after several pints, of the inn's finest bitter ale, the two men left the pub just before closing time, to go and share out their catch in the churchyard. They clambered over the wall and emptied the sacks onto a patch of grass between the wall, and the gravestone of a long dead gamekeeper.

As they began to count a local on inebriated feet was passing and overheard the two men sorting out their catch. "Let's see, why don't you have that one and I will take this one."

The man was horrified, fear then terror enveloped him and his inebriated feet sobered up and carried him at top speed to the police station in Newbridge on Wye, where he hammered on the door. The constable was about to go to bed and had to put his boots back on before opening the door. The now, stressed, horrified man was gasping for air and struggled to speak. "Constable, you have to come as fast as you can to Llanafan Churchyard." He stopped to breathe and the constable was about to ask why when the statement continued. "The lord and the devil are counting out the bodies, you have to come and do something about it."

The constable was skeptical, however he knew that he should do his duty and investigate. He placed his helmet on his head, made sure he had his handy truncheon and then took out his police issue bicycle from a shed behind the station. The informant was helped onto the bar of the bike and the constable pedaled their way back to the churchyard.

An eerie mist had begun to descend, an owl screeched and a lone fox in the distance, barked. The man and policeman crept up to the churchyard wall.

The two poachers were coming to the end of their sharing. "Well, this seems to be the last of them." Observed one.

"No, they are not," said the other, "what about those two on the other side of the wall?"

Panic seized the informant and policeman. They mounted up and peddled away at such a speed as would intimidate the competitors in a French cycle race. They didn't slow down even on the hills. It is said that early the next morning they were seen, still pedaling their way, passing through Hay on Wye, on their way into England, not even stopping to read a book.

For clarification "sniving" is a term used to describe a large moving mass of animals or people. "A tidy few" is a term used for a lesser number.

Hay-on-Wye is a town on the English Welsh border that is laden with books. Every shop, garage, movie theatre, chapel, church and castle is stacked with books of every description. The town is also known as the venue of the Hay festival which has a worldwide reputation.

SPRING

I am sitting here in a world of spring
A blue sky day full of birds that sing.
The leaves are sprouting it's green they bring
To take my heart and give it wing.

A scene exposed from winter's white
Recovered from the cooler night.
The warming days give insects flight
As the sun comes north to give us light.

It is the world that melts the will
The stream that flows through nearby rill.
A sunlit slope of a distant hill,
My senses surrounded to give me fill.

From swelling bulbs the world takes bloom.
The farmer's ready, the land to groom.
Our summers weaved from a springing loom.
For in the joy of spring there is no gloom.

The following are a selection of four poems written by my niece Cassie Powell, Tremaen.

A LONELY FEELING

A Lonely Feeling
From deep within.
Where did it come from?
Where did it begin?

An Empty Feeling
From deep inside.
A Feeling so strong
Impossible to hide.

A Lost Feeling
From deep in my head.
A feeling so confusing
The words can't be said.

A Broken Feeling
From deep in my heart.
A feeling from no-where
How did it start?

A Hurt Feeling
From deep in my soul
A feeling Unbearable
Too heavy to control

A Lonely Feeling
From deep within.
Where did it come from?
Where did it begin?

WILL LOVE EVER FIND ME

Will Love ever find me?
Said the voices in my head,
As I lie awake lonely
Crying in my Bed.

Will Love ever find me?
Or is it just not meant to be,
I refuse to believe
There's no one made for me.

Will Love ever find me?
Or am I looking too much,
For that loving feeling
For that tender touch.

Will love ever find me?
Or am I searching too hard,
For the romantic flowers
For that Valentines card.

Will Love ever find me?
No one can say,
But I will hold on to hope
That it will find me some day

DO NOT JUDGE ME

Do not judge me,
Because of my quirky weird ways,
Do not judge me,
Because the way I live my days.

Do not judge me,
With your vile nasty tongue,
Do not judge me,
Just look what you've become.

Do not judge me,
Because I don't run with the crowd,
Do not judge me,
Because I'm very proud.

Do not judge me,
Because I'm the way I'm meant to be
Do not judge me,
Because what I am is me.

MAKES YOU THINK

A whole story captured in one day
How did this poor man end up alone in this way?
No one there to gently pack up his things,
To watch him fly away with his angel wings.

A passport, a Christmas card all in the skip.
A life thrown away to end up on the tip.
A brand new coat hangs on the bedroom door
Surely this poor man deserved a little more.

Love letter's that I shouldn't really have read
The words so beautiful, could not be better said
She loved him and wanted to be with him forever
A reply never sent, read how he regretted it forever.

A half eaten meal still on his dinner plate
How could this poor man be left in such a state?
A bible, which seemed to be well read.
How did this happen? 'He died alone in his bed'

CLIMATE CHANGE

The planet goes through cycles of warming up and cooling down.
Warming is the recent trend that has been extensively observed.
Its runaway acceleration is brought about by efforts unreserved.
We dig up the dead of passed on life to give ourselves some crown.
Leave scars around our world of all the dug up dead to drown.
A healing process does its best when nothing is preserved.
Air contaminated without restraint when burning death is served.
The sun's rays trapped deflected by a tainted, atmospheric gown.

Two seventy parts per million for a hundred thousand years,
Increased by forty two percent in the three hundred just gone by.
The fossils burned can give us brightness to scare away our fears.
All the brightness outruns our natural world and leaves us in a lie.
Life smothered by heat and pollution should bring us all to tears.
Therefore we have to ponder and boldly ask the reason why.

WIND POWER

Fight against the turbine to save a harmless scene?
Prevent the blade of progress that provides a better need.
As time spins out for seas and pretty lands of green
The enemy is in the air the result of all our greed.

The ally in the scene should it never be allowed?
A sensible obstruction that reduces other means.
To prevent the melting of the poles should never be avowed?
Should we sacrifice those blades that could save our pretty scenes?

Although we see offence when we gaze across the hills
We do not see demise that is hidden in our skies.
The true nature of our planet that needs its normal chills,
We deny the cleaner way and do nothing as it dies.

All the winds that pass us by around our pretty globe
Have all the power we would ever need to keep us in a smile.
Why, blow away the energy that could save the verdant robe?
And find offense at a clean machine and not the really vile.

Look to lands that are stripped of life to garner C O two.
Oil, coal and tar sands dug out, our planet it does offend,
When clean alternatives in our hands are never given due.
We should never lose the opportunity to let our planet mend.

The following is a comic sketch written for the Na Fianna Irish players and played in Chicago in 2003.

TWO BRIDES FOR TWO COUSINS

NARRATOR
They say it is a waste of time to send coal to Old Newcastle.
Because, Newcastle, has plenty of its own, and doesn't need the hassle.
So, would it be a waste in Ireland to hold an Irish Fest.
Much better in America where the Irish show their best.
And from Ireland to America the Irish often come.
To visit distant relatives to see what they've become.
So we open in the Murphy house, in good old USA.
They are sitting in the living room where the conversations underway.

SCENE ONE

ANDERS
You know, if we were in the old country our Willie would be married off by now to one of them computer analyst girls.

KIRSTEN
Being single as long as he has he'd be a priest or even a bishop over there and I'd be as proud of him as my old Irish great grandmother would have been. God rest her soul.

WILLIE
Where am I going to find a computer Annie and why an Annie list. What would be wrong with looking in a Jane list or a Mary list. I'll tell you now if I find a woman I will be so desperate that I won't care if the girl's not on any list at all. (Anders shakes his head).

KIRSTEN
(Who is now reading the Irish Gazette) It says here that there are a lot of young American men getting brides from the old country. There is a

special service to make arrangements and everything. Red haired beauties, farmers daughters from Limerick and Cork. Now one of those girls would be ideal for our Willie.

WILLIE

I bet it would cost a lot to get one. I don't want an ugly one.. I've been down town and I've seen what they cost. Even the ugly ones are expensive.

ANDERS

Don't you be telling tales like that in front of your mother. You should be more careful. Those people transmit those DVD's or whatever they call them.

KIRSTEN

We won't worry about no bridal service. I'll call my cousin in Limerick. Her boy, Timmy, will be coming over for the Irish Fest we could send the money and have him bring a bride with him and the only service you'll have to worry about is the one for the wedding.

ANDERS

Well, get on the phone and let's get this thing rolling. Wow, this is a great idea. I wonder if they take tradeins. (Laughs)

KIRSTEN

Anders, what a thing to say. You'd better be careful or I'll be trading you in. Not that I'd ever get much for you.

ANDERS

Okay, okay, I was just joking. Make the call.

KIRSTEN

(Picks up the phone and dials) Is that you Kathleen? .. I'm fine, yes... Yes we still have a bit of snow. .. Is your Timmy still coming over for the fest... Oh, good we'll have a room ready for him...Yes, I'm sure he is... I was looking in the paper and I see there are a lot brides being brought to

America.. They do, but it seems they like them from the old country best... Yes, so could Timmy bring a bride over for our Willie. We would pay the expenses, of course, and he's going to make a great groom... How many? Just the one, do you think he's some kind of an Arabian...all right Kathleen, .. yes it was good talking to you too... yes, and we'll meet him at the airport.. Bye. (Hangs up). Well, that's settled. Willie, your cousin Timmy is going to bring a bride over for you when he comes over for the fest.

WILLIE

What does she look like?

KIRSTEN

They haven't found her yet, I've only just put in the order. I'm sure she'll be beautiful. A farmers daughter, Willie, from Ireland. She'll be hard working and a good cook.

ANDERS

It doesn't matter, he'll get what he's given. But, there again, perhaps she'll come with a thirty day guarantee and if we don't like her we can exchange her for a new one.

KIRSTEN

Anders, that will do, going through this once will be enough.

END SCENE ONE

NARRATOR

When you contact mother cultures, communication is a strain.
Because sometimes conversations are not always very plain.
Telephone calls at a distance are not always really clear
And can create confusion for all the loved ones dear.
When relatives get calls, and the static interferes,
It's like talking to a man whose belly's full of beer.

**So to the Murphy house, in Ireland, where the family is relaxed.
And wouldn't they be better off if the phone call had been faxed.**

SCENE TWO

PATRICK

You know, if our Timmy keeps on going to America he'll be winding up
with one of them tall, handsome Annies over there.

TIMMY

I don't know if I'll find a tall, handsome Annie. And what would be wrong
with a short handsome Jane or a short handsome Mary. I'll tell you now
if I find a handsome woman over there I wont care what her name is or
how tall she is. (Patrick shakes his head).

KATHLEEN

He spends more time in America than he spends in church. He met a
priest the other day and went right up to him and asked where his body
piercings were and was he after getting himself some tatoos. Then he
asked him for his autograph. The poor man is still in shock.

TIMMY

I thought he was out of that heavy metal band "The Cast Iron Bishops."
He looked just like the man, still in costume and stuff.

PATRICK

There were a few of those kind of bishops about when I was a young
man.

KATHLEEN

(Who is now reading the Irish Gazette) There are a lot of Irish lads that
are finding brides in America and they say it's not a lot of trouble
arranging the weddings. It says here that a lot of them are blonde girls

from the valleys of California. You should take a good look around you over there and come up with one of them girls for yourself.

PATRICK

And don't pick the first one you meet. Make sure the blonde is real first. Perhaps I should go with you. I know a little bit about selecting young ladies, look at your mother.

KATHLEEN

I'm not going to let you go to America to examine young girls. What do you think I am? I remember the kind of girl I was. Timmy can select his own girl and it doesn't matter what color her hair is.

PATRICK

Alright, I'm sorry, I was just joking with you.

KATHLEEN

(The phone rings, she answers.) Oh, it's you Kirsten. How nice. How are you?... What's the weather like with you? (She covers mouth piece) There's a lot of sizzle on the line. (Then continues).. Yes, he is... Oh, your very kind...Yes. He's looking forward to it... (Hand over mouth piece) She says there are a lot of bridles being taken over to America. (continues) Don't you have them over there.. Oh well that's nice.. How many of them would you like Kirsten?.. Oh, just the one then...It's nice talking to you... We'll let you know when he's flying... Bye. (Hangs up) Well, now it seems that cousin Willie has got himself a horse, an Arabian, she says and she wants Timmy to bring out a bridle for it when he goes over to the Fest. It must be a fine horse, because he has a groom for it and everything.

END SCENE TWO

NARRATOR

The finest bridle anywhere was bought for Timmy's trip.
And then, a long flight on a DC10 without a sign of kip.

We have now moved through the airport where Timmy's underway.
His bags are packed and ready, and there's little left to say.
It's goodbye, to all the family, before he boards the plane
And leaves his sunny Ireland, for Chicago and the rain.
Now Timmy is excited, as the plane comes in to land.
He imagines he's a president, who gets greeted by a band.
He walks up through the corridors to the officials at the gate.
To the uniformed obstruction that can make you very late.
He meets the customs agent, who is working for the flag.
He pulls our Timmy over. "Let's see what's in your bag?"

SCENE THREE

(Timmy comes through the door and is met by a customs official.)

OFFICIAL

This way , Sir, please. Let's see what's in the bag, Sir, please?
(Timmy opens bag and takes out contents including the bridle.)

OFFICIAL

(Glances at other items and then points at bridle). What's that and
what's it for?

TIMMY

It's for an Arabian.

OFFICIAL

What did you say, Sir?

TIMMY

I said it was for an Arabian.

OFFICIAL

(Startled) OK,Sir, who is this Arabian and what kind of weapon is this
holster for? Do you have the weapon with you?

TIMMY

I don't have a weapon, it's not for a weapon it's for an Arabian I said.

OFFICIAL

If this is not a holster for a weapon what are all the straps for and (Pointing to the bit.) what's that part there?

TIMMY

It's a bit.

OFFICIAL

A bit of what?

TIMMY

It's not a bit of anything. It's a bit for your horse's mouth.

OFFICIAL

(Upset). That's it pal, I'm arresting you, you're going back to where you came from. Goldarned terrorists. (Marches Timmy through the door.)

END SCENE THREE

NARRATOR

They interrogated Timmy, and he stood there just aghast.
There was no sign of Al Qaeda, or Osama, in his past.
The relatives to greet him, were pacing to and fro.
But poor Timmy is deported, back to Ireland he must go.
They weren't sure if he'd landed, or caught the plane at all,
And tried to solve the problem, but knew not who to call.
So back home, to the phone to wait, they had no further clues.
But soon enough they got a call, and heard the awful news.
Now once again we will drop in to hear the shocking tale.
Is this disaster all the truth, or did the system fail.

SCENE FOUR

KIRSTEN

Can you imagine that, poor cousin Timmy deported for smuggling weapons equipment for the Arabs. And he insulted a customs official. Kathleen was horrified when I told her what had happened. Oh, that poor family. I don't know why he'd want to do a thing like that. I know gas is expensive over there, but he'd hardly do a thing like that for the oil.

ANDERS

Perhaps it was the bride he was bringing over, put him up to it. I wouldn't put it past any of those young equal righters that are about today.

KIRSTEN

When I talked to the authorities they said they didn't think he had an accomplice. What they did say was; that the package he had with him is under armed guard. Poor girl, there she is, her first time in America and finds herself under armed guard. What will she think of us?

ANDERS

Well, perhaps she is an Arabian girl and they are trying to find out who her contacts are. If she's wearing a veil they're probably trying to find out who she is and what she looks like.

WILLIE

Why would Timmy bring me an Arabian girl from Ireland? I didn't know there were any Arabs in Ireland. There are no deserts or anything. It's not as if they have camels over there.

KIRSTEN

(Phone rings) Hello... Yes it is. (Long pause)..OK but we could have come back to the airport, you know... Two or three days. Oh my God... OK bye. (She hangs up.) Oh, that poor girl. they said that she was an innocent package.

ANDERS

They must have got her burqa off. I've never seen an Irish girl with one of them. Anyway, what's going to happen to her now?

KIRSTEN

It seems that she is being released and they are sending her here in a delivery truck and it will take two or three days for her to get here. What a thing to do to a young girl. It doesn't matter if she is an Arabian girl this is no way to treat her. Her first time in the country and she has to spend three days in a delivery truck being driven by a greasy man with his "hammer down" and shouting out "ten four" all the time. They wouldn't do that to an American girl, I can tell you.

ANDERS

Well, did they tell you what her name is?

KIRSTEN

No. They just kept referring to her as a package. I tell you I don't know what the world is coming to.

END SCENE FOUR

NARRATOR

Now back again to Ireland, to the home in Limerick.
The family's very shocked, and are feeling really sick.
"The bloody boy is off his head." our Patrick seems to think.
He couldn't understand it, was this because of drink.

SCENE FIVE

KATHLEEN

Poor Timmy and him just after smuggling weapons to the Arabs.
Somebody must have put him up to it.

PATRICK

Poor Timmy my arse. When I get a hold of him I'll kill him. Weapons for the Arabs indeed, I'll never be able to hold my head up in town again. It won't be long before the police'll be around here wanting to know who his friends are. My God. Have you seen those friends of his. They all have these metal objects sticking out of them. One had a big brass curtain ring sticking out of his nose. Another, had one in his eyebrow and I have heard they have them in other places that I don't care to mention. They have more hardware hanging off them than an over stocked tinker. (pause) Don't you tell anyone that he belongs to me. (pause) I might have gone a long way to sympathize if it was for the IRA he did it.

KATHLEEN

Oh my God. They'll have him in jail on bread and water for years. The shame of it. We'll have to move to England.

PATRICK

He must have been drunk or a little touched, because I know for a fact he doesn't know any Arabs.

(Enter Timmy He seems quite cheerful.)

TIMMY

Hello, Mother, hello, Da. They deported me, you Know. They wouldn't let me stay and I heard that they will ship the bridle on to the cousins in America.

PATRICK

Deported, deported. It's bloody shot you should be. Smuggling weapons to the Arabs indeed. I've a good mind to shoot you myself. What the divil came over you and what are you doing here? I thought you'd been arrested. I thought you were in custody. Under armed guard

KATHLEEN

Oh, my God. You've escaped jail, haven't you? You shouldn't have done it Timmy, you'll have to turn yourself in again. We didn't raise you to be dishonest.

TIMMY

Will ya shut up. It was all a big mistake. They thought I was smuggling equipment for weapons because the eejit at the airport didn't know what a bridle was. I told him it was for an Arabian and they arrested me, interrogated me and put me back on the plane. They thought I was some sort of terrorist. They couldn't prove anything there and sent me back to Ireland to be reprocessed. When I landed they told me that it had all been a mistake. But I have fantastic news for you.

PATRICK

This had better be bloody good after all you've put us through. Your cousins in America have been worried sick.

TIMMY

(Goes to the door and beckons for someone to come in. Enter a beautiful young girl.) Mother, Da. This is Annie, I met her on the plane on the way back from America. She's from Dublin. And I know this is a bit quick but we have fallen in love.

ANNIE

It's lovely to meet you. Timmy has told me all about you. (They stare into one another's eyes.)

END SCENE FIVE

NARRATOR

For the embarrassed airport agents, they ought to say a mass.
As for that old customs man, they put him out to grass.
The bridle then was gathered up, and shipped off in a truck.
The authorities had realized, this thing was just bad luck.
So we return again to America, where three whole days have passed.
The waiting will soon be over, and she'll arrive at last.
Oh, what a disappointment. Where is this bride to be?
She was hardly in that little box, as everyone could see.

After all these expectations, had this bridal woman bailed?
Or should they blame the messenger, for the delivery that has failed.

SCENE SIX

ANDERS

Where's Willie?

KIRSTEN

I've told him to go and put a nice jacket on and get himself ready to meet his bride. I am certain that it's today that she'll arrive. It' a mothers instinct, you know.

(There is a Knock on the door. Kirsten is on her feet in a second and opens the door. At the door is a delivery person (girl) with a package.)

GIRL

Delivery for Willie Murphy.

KIRSTEN

Where is the girl?

GIRL

What girl maam?

KIRSTEN

The girl, the bride, from Ireland that's supposed to be delivered to us from the airport.

GIRL

I have no idea what you are talking about. All I have is a package. (she looks at clip board) It contains a bridle for a horse.

KIRSTEN

What do we need a bridle for, we don't have a horse. You've made a mistake, I ought to smack you one, you were supposed to deliver a bride not a bridle. How stupid can you get?

ANDERS

(On his feet and approaches the door.) For goodness sake Kirsten she's
just a delivery person. You can't abuse the messenger. It's not her fault.
Ask her in for goodness sake.   (The girl is invited in.)

ANDERS

Come in. Sit down there, and tell us what is going on.

GIRL

All I know is that an Irish man by the name of (Looks at clip board.)
Timmy Murphy.

ANDERS

Yes, that's one of our cousins in Ireland.

GIRL

He was coming to visit you and was bringing this bridle which is in this
package here. It said that you had requested he bring it over on his trip
to the US. That is all I know and normally I don't get that much
information.

KIRSTEN

It was supposed to be a bride he was bringing not a bridle. This is terrible
and I've been worried about a poor Irish girl or an Arabian girl who
doesn't even exist.

(Willie enters with nice jacket and stares at the delivery girl and she in
turn stares at him. Their gaze is locked. Kirsten and Anders look back and
fore at the young couple.)

WILLIE

Annie. Is that you?

ANNIE (GIRL)

William. I never thought I would ever see you again.

WILLIE

Mom, Dad, this is Annie. We haven't seen each other since high school. Wow, Annie you look fabulous.

ANDERS

(Taking Kirsten aside.) You don't have any more to say or wish for. Let's leave well alone. The bride has delivered herself.

END SCENE SIX

NARRATOR

After all this great confusion the cousins got their Brides.

They decided not to hold the weddings, across the ocean tides.

Because after all the troubles, they'd leave air planes well alone.

They sent each other greetings, and chanced it on the phone.

Although in separate countries, it was a double marriage.

And away to spend their honeymoons, aboard a horse and carriage,

Happy ever after, their lives they'd surely spend.

And of course this saga's over, and our story's at an end.

MEMORIES

Oh, Dylan, where are you now, boy bach?
Long gone. Laugharne, misses you.
The Heron priested shores are lonely.

Would you amble down to Brown's
And a pint of best to toast the world of words?
Would you reacquaint in the farmlands of Carmarthen?

Would you gather stars above the Towey River?
And dip your toes in the rippling tides of *your* Wales.
Would you tear another stanza from Fern Hill?

Would you shipwreck in that milky wood?
Fight for Rosie Probert in your dreams?
Or board a charabanc that will never reach Porthcawl?

Can we not be gentle after your goodnight?
We will always rage against the dying of your light
And search the wisdom of your verse.

Perhaps you left us with enough
But oh, how much more it could have been.
Will we ever find ways to live in your imagination?

RAPTOR

Peregrine
The traveler
Stooping through time.
Natures flashing sky cleaver
With precise and ready eyes.
Taking the prey with talons sharp
With a feathered cloud a speedy death.
Plucked and devoured with hooked beak.
With ready eye finely tuned
Sliced sky caught meal
Time has stooped
The wanderer
Conquerer.

A DART TEAM

The Irish Well was an early nineties icon of bohemian extravagance and Irish culture, situated in St Paul's, Midway area. In actual fact the exact center of the Twin Cities Metropolitan area was marked by a brass plaque set in the floor in the passage of entry.

It was a cultural center, indeed. Live music, storytelling, and poetry was wonderfully stirred, espoused and served up by the faithful patrons. There were also games, a small pool table, and electronic dartboards.

Two dart boards had been placed in a half circle room, attached to the main dining room, and entertainment area, under an amicable contract with a local vending company.

They were not used extensively and the vending company removed one of them, as two were not monetarily viable. A man with a large dolly wheeled away one of the machines.

It was two weeks later when the man returned with his dolly and another machine. He smiled. "I will set this up for the 'Blind Dart League' they will be here on Tuesday evening."

Blind people, playing darts? It would be easy to conjure up major safety concerns. The man was obviously joking. He had a spare machine and needed somewhere to keep it, until it was needed elsewhere.

On the following Tuesday evening a Metro Mobility bus showed up and discharged ten guide dogs with blind human beings attached. I happened to be in the entry passage and stared open mouthed at the canine led invasion. A man that was being pulled along by the leading dog sensed my presence and asked in a loud voice. "Where's the dartboard?"

This has to be a major practical joke, I thought, and it wasn't the sort of practical joke that would be beyond several of my current patrons.

I answered. "You, er, um, want to know where the dartboard, is?"

"Yea, man, we are here to play darts."

I led them through to the dart boards, visualizing a line of ambulances outside ready to take a continual stream of customers to the hospital, that had been struck with wayward flying darts.

After indicating the location of the board I watched as each of them ran their hands over it making approving noises, and then out of their pockets they pulled boxes that contained darts. The dogs were obedient when asked to settle on the long Nagga Hide seat that ran under the curved, mirrored wall. A guide dog was privileged, as being the only live animal allowed entry to any pub and restaurant in the Twin Cities if not in the entire seven state area.

The first dart was thrown. I had stood well back. I am a sighted person, although, I do have to wear spectacles and I can throw a reasonably straight dart. However my dart playing skills were pretty miserable compared to these players. That first dart went straight into double top and I was shocked when the board itself announced the score. "Double Twenty."

Was this a lucky throw? Certainly not. There were very few misses from these players. It seemed that some bright individual had decided to invent a talking dart board just for sightless people.

I had often heard good players over the years bragging. "Oh, I could play that man blindfold."

The blind players gave every sighted player that opportunity; they carried blindfolds for such challenges.

IF I COULD TRAVEL TIME

If I could travel time
I would visit friends gone by.
I would show them where to tread on a journey through a life.

If I could travel time
I would see history as it happens.
I'd come back and read the books and see if they are right.

If I could travel time
I would reach into the future.
So that I would know the way ahead and avoid the world's mistakes.

If I could travel time
I would find all the finest foods
And all the meals I loved the best I'd go back and eat again.

If I could travel time
I would find the best of fun.
All the worst I would pass by and never lose my smile.

If I could travel time
I would make a better world.
Make sure to banish pain and keep us all quite safe.

If you could travel time
Would you do right for all the world?
Could you travel for the good and the welfare of us all?

This is the poem that Marged Evans writes and recites in Troedrhiwdalar Eisteddfod. The third book. The Timeless Cavern – Marged Evans and the Pebbles of Distance

KLINGONS

There was an extensive basement ballroom in the Irish Well. It was used for dinners, concerts, balls and other events. The local Star Trek fan club would hold mini, one day, conventions there two or three times a year, on Sundays. I would set up the room so that they were able to self cater the event. This worked out well and gave me a chance to take some time off before I had to open for the evening.

When I was ready to open up the upstairs bar and restaurant, at five, I would shout down the stairs to let them know that refreshments would soon be available.

Having done this for one of these events I had placed myself behind the bar and readied the cocktail condiments. I glanced up when I heard footsteps approaching down the hall. My eyes widened when I saw what was coming into the restaurant.

Ten Klingons settled themselves around the small peninsular bar. They were perfectly made up in every detail as if they had walked right off the set of Star Trek itself.

They carried their weapons with them including, Mek'leth's, Kut'luch's and those large curved scything weapons that they called Bat'leth's. All their eyes were on me as I carefully looked each of these fierce individuals over. It was then that I realized that I could not let this pass without comment.

I straightened up to make myself look as large as possible. A futile effort as every one of them, females included, were twice my size. I banged my hand down on the bar and at the top of my voice I made my announcement. "Alright, you lot, I know your reputation for violence in this man's galaxy, weapons on the table in the corner." I pointed to a table in a far corner of the room.

I could see it going through their minds. "Oh kuhle, he's into this." They stood as one and filed to the corner of the room and cluttered up the table with weaponry and returned to their seats and waited for what was to come next.

"Are you hungry?" I asked. "Are you here to eat?"

They all nodded and I stared at each of them in turn once more. "Alright, there won't be any of your Gok here. You will have Irish, Warrior Stew, and you will like it."

They all nodded, and then were duly served, and I noticed that for Klingons their table manners were quite formal. It seemed to me that they were a lot more civilized than I had been led to believe.

A CHRISTMAS DAY

She vigorously tore the paper from the large box.
Sprigs of holly with bright red berries and Santa ripped in half.
The shredded wrappings strewn around the room.
That decorative outer covering was in the way of her intent.
What were the contents that deserved this eager scramble?
She didn't know it, but it had to be amazing.
Surely it was magical, it was written on her face.
Most assuredly the best of presents were hidden in that box.
The shielding cardboard split apart and the contents were revealed.
Santa's image was torn asunder, but to her he had delivered.

The joy that gifts this day is the best for those who give.
There is true happiness in the heart of a care free little girl.
How far beyond the dreams and wishes can someone really go?
In childhood it is possible long before we grow.
If only we could take it with us before our sun goes down.

THE DUCK RACE

The Royal Welsh Show in my home town is four July days of crowded, agricultural bliss. Every farmer and his or her relatives from all over Wales, and the rest of the British Isles descend into that salmon rivered town to see the finest livestock on the planet displayed in honoured splendor in the show's grand arena of champions.

Every imaginable exhibition is lined up along the aisles of this summer time extravagance; a wonderful place to meet old friends from long ago, and other times and places.

It was on a visit there several years ago that I was approached by a smartly dressed man wearing a pressed shirt, a tie, and a dark suit. His shoes had been shiny; however, the dust of the day had taken its toll. He had come out from behind a table that was piled up with promotional materials for various fund raising organizations.

He came right up to my side, and then took some very furtive glances in several directions, and then he leaned into my ear and softly asked. "Do you want to buy a duck?"

I stared for a moment, taking in what he had just asked. "No thank you." I replied.

His eyebrows went up as if horrified by my straight forward answer. "He's a fast duck."

"That's very nice," I said, "I still don't want to buy it."

"Oh, but you should, he is entered for the big race, you see."

"Well, if he is that good, why do you want to sell him?"

"Oh, that is because I have decided that the money from the sale will be donated to charity."

"Well, that sounds very generous. So where is this duck?"

"Ooh, you can't see him he's in training."

"In training?" Was my incredulous response.

"Yes, in training for the big race."

"So you are trying to sell a duck sight unseen."

"I know, but he has a marvelous reputation."

"I must say I am impressed. I would consider buying it except for the fact that I live in America."

"Ooh, you wouldn't be able to take him there. He would miss the race."

"Well, that's the end of that then."

"No, no, no. You could still buy him."

"Alright," I said, "let's put this all together. You have a very fast racing, may I say, thoroughbred duck that you want to sell to me? He is entered for a big race and I can't see him because he is in training. Not only that, if I were to buy him I wouldn't be able to take him back to America with me. So just out of interest, how much do you want for this amazing duck?"

"A pound."

"A pound. Only a pound, for this highly trained, high speed duck. That's about a dollar fifty in America. I was considering its purchase and I had imagined having to take out a loan to buy it. But, for only a pound, I'll pay for it now."

It turned out that the duck I was buying was a plastic duck, with its own personal number. This duck at a later date would be tipped into the River Wye with hundreds of others with personal numbers. The first duck to cross the line further downstream would win its owner a hundred pounds, a useful sum.

Only a Welshman would go to that much trouble to raise a pound for charity and deliver a sales pitch that could be considered as being worth many times the value of the return.

A few weeks later back in America I get a phone call from my father. We exchanged the usual pleasantries and then he said. "Your name is in the Brecon and Radnor."

This was a surprise and so I asked. "What have I supposed to have done, now?"

He hesitated for a second. "Well, I am not sure. It says that you have won a hundred pounds in a duck race."

I was stunned. My very fast, highly trained, thoroughbred racing duck had won his race. I explained to father how it had been sold and further explained that it was a plastic duck. His response was. "Well, I'll be jiggered."

About four weeks later I met Ian Brown the Headmaster of Builth Wells High School, at the Twin Cities Airport, escorting five or six students from the school on an exchange visit.

Ian had the distinction of being the adopted son of James Herriot of "All Creatures Great and Small" fame. On seeing me he smiled and spoke with his Yorkshire accent in full flow. "Ooh, John Dingley, I see you won a duck race. What are you going to do with the 'undred pounds?"

Now, Ian Brown had a "Cardi" approach when raising money for the good of the school, no doubt because, coming from Yorkshire he had been raised close to Scotland.

I smiled. "Well, this is what I can do. The hundred pounds should stay in Wales so the school can have it as a donation; however, there are two things I would like you to do in exchange."

"What might those be?"

"Well, first I would like you to use some of the money to place a notice board in the school listing experts, with their contact information, in the various hobbies and activities that students might be interested in. Any monies left over you can use as you wish."

"That's a good idea. I will see that that gets done."

"Secondly, I want you to find that duck, and get it for me so that I can pick it up on my next visit home."

"I will make enquiries and do what I can."

A few months later I had returned to Wales and marched into Ian's office at the High School. "Hello Ian. Where's my duck?"

He answered with concern. "Ooh, I have had a bit of a problem finding that duck. It seems that the man you have to contact is a man called Donald, in Llangammarch Wells."

"Are you kidding, Donald the duck man?"

He chuckled. "When I heard you were coming over I got his phone number for you. But, you will like to know; a notice board was made and is now on the wall for the students to see."

I called Donald from Ian's office and he informed me that it was a John Williams I had to see for a duck. He told me that I would find him at the fire station in Llanwrtyd Wells. I drove out to Llanwrtyd and found the fire station and entered. There was a lone man there who was cleaning the floor with a very noisy pressure washer. I tapped him on the shoulder. He turned.

I loudly asked. "John Williams?"

"Yes."

"Good. I have come for my duck."

He stared. "What did you say?"

"I said. I have come for my duck."

"Hang on a minute." He stopped the machine. "What is it you want?"

"My duck."

Welsh people are not good at giving totally blank stares but this one was. "I don't know nothing about no duck."

I said. "You are John Williams, aren't you?"

"Yes, I am."

"You were supposed to know about a duck."

It was then that he realized that there was a bit of a mix up. "Oh, no, I am not John Williams from here. I am John Williams from Llandrindod Wells. I am on loan."

I asked. "Where is the other John Williams."

"I couldn't tell you, and I don't know where he lives."

It seemed that tracking down my duck was more complicated than I had imagined. Not knowing where to find the other John Williams, and not having a phone number I returned to Builth Wells and the school. The number was found and the real John Williams asked me to return to Llanwrtyd Wells and meet him on the station road there. This I did and I was given my racing duck.

I returned to America with my winning, high speed duck, and as it had done very well in the big race I made sure that its time in America would be spent in retirement. Of course, there would be the occasional round of exercise in the bathtub.

A "Cardi" is a person from the county of Cardigan. Many years ago it was explained to me how frugal a Cardigan person was. The explanation was illustrated by the following story.

The police had recovered a body from the River Thames, in London, and on examination it was found that the individual had been dead for some two weeks. There was no identification as to who the person was, or where he had come from.

A constable on the scene pointed out the possibility that the dead man could have been in London for a Wales versus England Rugby match, that had taken place two weeks previously. So there was a chance that the man was from Wales, and the constable was asked if there was any way to find out.

The constable thought for a second or two and then said that there was a test that could be carried out and was asked, by his superior officer to make the test.

The constable, who himself was from Cardigan, not wanting to risk his own money borrowed a penny from his superior officer and placed it in the dead man's open hand. The decaying fingers on the dead hand closed over the penny thus proving that the man was not only from Wales, but from Cardigan itself.

Incidentally, I have met many a Cardi and found them to be cordial, convivial and not ungenerous.

Inspired when I read the following account:

"In 1840, 6-year old Susan Reece said *'I have been below six or eight months and I don't like it much. I come here at six in the morning and leave at six at night. When my lamp goes out or I am hungry I go home. I haven't been hurt yet'*. Her mission was to open and close the ventilator at Plymouth Colliery, Merthyr Tydfil"

SUSAN REECE 1840

I am six years old.
I go with Dad before the light
To join others at the pit.
It is there at six we go crowding down below.
"I don't like it much."

I work the doors down in the mine.
Open close, open close, open close
To let in the air so we all can breathe.
All dark long, one tiny stop to eat, with dirty hands.
"I don't like it much."

Six at night our shift is done.
A black clanking ride back to the top,
The light of day has come and gone.
My sunshine has been taken and joy has gone away.
"I don't like it much."

Mam helps me clean away the dust,
I am tired, I would love to play.
A little bread and milk before I go to sleep
And I dream of doors, open close, open close, open close.
"I don't like it much."

The air I move it is not good,
For it flows through the smelly bad
The stinkdamp and the afterdamp,
The blackdamp low and firedamp waiting for a spark.
"I don't like it much."

Every day til Sunday, six to six below.
Others just like me tush the carts of coal,
Little boys, chained and blooded to their work.
We have no tree or bright green field or pretty flower's smell.
"I don't like it much."

They pay a penny for my work.
I give it to my Dad for food.
He promises a sweetie so he can see me smile.
All my days are dark and dirty coal and always I'm afraid.
"I don't like it much."

There is no work on Sunday,
Mam takes me to the chapel, where we sing.
The preacher shouts of sin and hell,
And my work the will of God, I wish he'd change his mind.
"I don't like it much."

I will be seven soon.
My work it has not stopped.
They say I'm lucky to work below.
There's hunger in my tummy and my lamp is all but out.
"I haven't been hurt yet."

I wanted to find out more about this little girl and had Richard Meredith
a master genealogist research her life and family. See the following.

Susan Reece (Susannah Rees) became 7 years old in 1840.

In 1840 she was working in the Plymouth Colliery, Merthyr Tydfil . By the time she was seven years old child labour laws had changed and she didn't work again in the mine until she was ten years old. She was still working in the mine at the age of seventeen. Her father died in a mining accident in 1861. He was Isaac Rees and married Ann Morgan in 1827.

Susannah had four sisters, Mary, Martha, Emma and Margaret.

In 1857 she married Evan Isaac Jones on the 28th November. Evan died ten years later leaving Susannah with six children. He died in a mining accident in the Ferndale Colliery when a fellow miner or miners exposed a naked flame of a safety lamp which set off an explosion that killed 178 miners. The children were, oldest to youngest, Elizabeth (was a laundress at the age of thirteen), Maryann, Margaret, Richard, Susannah and Evan Isaac (born after the death of his father).

In 1871 Susannah was working in an iron works. In 1881 Maryann, Richard and Evan were living with her. In 1891 she and Evan, who was a coal miner were living in Jackson Square Merthyr Tydfil. Next door was a man called Thomas Samuels who was from Llanafan Fawr, a parish featured in this book.

Susannah died in 1901 aged 68 years. Her last grandchild died in 1994. There are living descendants, some in Wales, some in England and some in Virginia, USA.

THE GO, GO, GO, TRAIN

There is a little village on the island of Anglesey at the end of the Menai Bridge. It has a name of some distinction that could have only been devised by a very large enthusiastic committee. It seems that not one modest name was sufficient and selected for unanimously. Every name put forward by all members of that committee was not left out or discarded. All the names were placed together in a free flowing conglomeration that became the very long extended name of Llanfairpwllgwyngyllgogerychwyrndrobwllllantysiliogogogoch.

It is not an isolated community by any means for running through the stone built, vibrant residences is a major railway line, one end of which is in the large city of London and the other end is in Anglesey's port town of Holyhead where ferried travelers to and from Ireland embark and disembark.

For many years British Rail employed English Guards to collect tickets and keep order on the trains and a part of their job was to announce the names of impending stations as the train proceeded with its journey.

A great difficulty presented itself to the guards and that was the pronunciation of the Welsh place names of the towns the train passed through. Many of the names were improperly pronounced and mangled in the process. Llanfairpwllgwyngyllgogerychwyrndrobwllllantysiliogogogoch, was one of these. However, not just one of the many, but because of the names length its announcement was never completed and was often followed with this statement in the best of BBC English.. "I'm awfully sorry, we have passed the station."

To alleviate the embarrassment, British Rail decided that the train would no longer stop or even attempt to stop in Llanfairpwllgwyngyllgogerychwyrndrobwllllantysiliogogogoch anymore.

Eventually, to assuage the complaints of the Welsh public, it was decided that only Welsh Guards would work the trains while they travelled through Wales. This was a major improvement, however the train did not stop in Llanfairpwllgwyngyllgogerychwyrndrobwllllantysiliogogogoch, because of some unjust oversight that has continued for many years.

Now, for a resident of Llanfairpwllgwyngyllgogerychwyrndrobwllllantysiliogogogoch, who wanted to travel by rail the unstopping train presented a problem. The only way to catch the train was to travel a dozen miles by car to a station further into Anglesey, where it did stop.

So whenever I, as a Llanfairpwllgwyngyllgogerychwyrndrobwllllantysiliogogogoch, resident, wished to travel to London on such, bi-yearly, trips to witness those great occasions when Wales played England at Twickenham in the Six Nations Rugby tournaments, I had to persuade my mother to drive me to the little station from Llanfairpwllgwyngyllgogerychwyrndrobwllllantysiliogogogoch, that was in the opposite direction to the way I wanted to go. I would board the train and then travel back through Llanfairpwllgwyngyllgogerychwyrndrobwllllantysiliogogogoch, on the way to see the much anticipated game in London.

On one particular happy occasion, a year when Wales won the rugby game and the Triple Crown I joined a smiling, joyous scrum of celebrators for the return journey to the victorious country. (Just an aside here, for clarification; Wales always beats England in these matches, however there are times when England scores more points.)

There I was amongst the leek jostling throng of this train journey, and as we travelled through England's 'Green and Pleasant Land', I would have the following, almost troubling thought. "It's a pity this train doesn't stop in Llanfairpwllgwyngyllgogerychwyrndrobwllllantysiliogogogoch."

Once we were into Wales following the change of guards at the border my thought became more frequent. It was during one of these that Big George, one of the guards and a man I knew, came into the carriage checking for tickets. He saw me as he looked down from his great height. To me he always seem to be about eight feet tall. I had never known him however, to be rarely more than friendly.

"John," he boomed, with his Welsh Chorus, sought after, bottom bass voice, "how are you boy? You was at the game, was you?"

I smiled up at him as I showed him my ticket. "Yes, and a grand game it was. Were you at the game?"

"No, I had to work, and I am always a little sad at missing the games. But, then again, see, I like to think that the train to and from the games couldn't run without me."

"Yes," I said, "and it's a pity it doesn't stop in Llanfairpwllgwyngyllgogerychwyrndrobwllllantysiliogogogoch, anymore."

He nodded. "Aye, it is a pity, indeed. It's the regulations, see, they won't allow us to stop." He had turned away to continue checking tickets, when he stopped and turned back. "Hang on a minute, I have an idea and although, I say it myself, it is a brilliant idea."

Just as he had finished that statement we heard an old, dusty voice that crackled from a giant leek in the corner of the carriage. George and I turned in its direction and we could hardly see through the leaves of this giant leek, but what we did see was a small piece of walnut wrinkled skin on a face of a man that wore a shepherd's flat cap. "It'll never 'appen." He said. "Ooh, no, it'll never 'appen, no, it'll never 'appen." Then he settled.

George continued with his idea. "John, I am a big man."

I smiled up at him. "Yes, you are."

"And you are not very big."

I smiled again. "True."

He continued. "If we could persuade the driver to slow the train down as we are coming into Llanfairpwllgwyngyllgogerychwyrndrobwllllantysiliogogogoch, I could hold you out the window and if you got your legs going, I could drop you off on the platform as we're going through the station. What do you think?"

I was elated. "Brilliant! Let's do it. Let's go and see the driver."

As we left the carriage, on the way to see the driver, the old shepherd in the corner livened up again. "It'll never 'appen. Ooh, no, it'll never 'appen, no, it'll never 'appen." The breath of his words were gently fluttering the leaves of his giant leek.

George and I were soon up at the front of the train where we approached Harry, the driver. Harry, was a careful looking man of exacting stature, his British Rail uniform, precisely pressed to a perfect fit.

"Harry," George boomed, "I have John by here, he is from Llanfairpwllgwyngyllgogerychwyrndrobwllllantysiliogogogoch."

And before George could say anymore, Harry, in his quick uniform felt he knew what was coming next and it would not be a perfect fit, and in a highly pitched North Walian accent spoke his objection. "How many times do I have to tell you, this train do no longer stop in Llanfairpwllgwyngyllgogerychwyrndrobwllllantysiliogogogoch, anymore. Regulations, can't do it."

George, interrupted this potential tirade before it could burst completely out of the man's uniform. "No, no, Harry, bach, we don't want you to stop the train, mun. We just wanted you to slow it down a bit so that I can hold John by the scruff of his neck out the window and drop him off on the platform as we go through, Llanfairpwllgwyngyllgogerychwyrndrobwllllantysiliogogogoch."

Harry, between glances at the rails ahead, making sure not to neglect his British Rail responsibility, looked George up and down. He started at the big man's feet and slowly moved up to the top of his head and then back down again. He turned to me and my size and height was taken in by one short flash of his deadly, serious eyes. "Alright, then, I will do it. But, be warned, mind, I am only going to slow the train down to fifty miles an hour from the usual eighty."

George, looked at me. "Will that be alright for you, John?"

"Yes, anything to get me home to

Llanfairpwllgwyngyllgogerychwyrndrobwllllantysiliogogogoch."

So back down the train to my carriage George and I went, to ready ourselves for my unconventional exit.

George cleared an area of people and leeks in front of one of the windows as Harry, true to his word, began slowing down the train. George's voice boomed out once more as he opened up the window. "Come on John, we'll soon be going through Llanfairpwllgwyngyllgogerychwyrndrobwllllantysiliogogogoch, start climbing out the window."

As I was scrambling through, so George could hold me outside in readiness, the old man was peering out from behind his jungle of leek, and his dusty voice crackled once again. "No, no, it'll never 'appen. Ooh, no, it'll never 'appen. No, it'll never 'appen."

I grinned at him. "You watch this, old man," I said, "it is going to happen any second, now."

The train was approaching the platform. George was holding me by the scruff of the neck. I was hanging outside the train window. George was booming once again over the clattering noise of the wheels on the rails. "Get your legs going, John, we are almost there."

My little legs were pedaling in the air as fast as I could make them. In a second the platform was there and George, let me go. I landed in full stride running up the platform endeavoring to slow down. It was wonderful, I was home in Llanfairpwllgwyngyllgogerychwyrndrobwllllantysiliogogogoch.

The train was soon picking up speed again and as the last carriage was passing me a hand reached out through a window and grabbed me by the scruff of the neck and pulled me back on board. As I landed back in the carriage I heard the voice of Wil, the other guard on the train. "Boy, John, you could have missed this train, we don't stop in Llanfairpwllgwyngyllgogerychwyrndrobwllllantysiliogogogoch anymore."

Footnote. Really, just another story.

This story was first told in the upper bar of the Park East Hotel in

Milwaukee, Wisconsin, in the late 1980's. Our theatre group was performing at Milwaukee's prestigious Irish Festival and as entertainers we got to party with the Irish Stars that were also performing there. The stars included The Chieftains, The Clancy Brother's, Chris O'Neill the Abbey and Broadway actor, and other entertainers of note, that included the stars of our dramatic group of actors that included, Kathie Luby, Dan Gleeson, Lar Burke and several others.

We had partied together each evening beginning on the Thursday. A room filled with dynamic entertainers all, as entertainers do, scrambling for attention and the opportunity to try out new ideas. It was great fun and always ended up with a round or two of "Your Noble Call." During each round Chris O'Neill would be called upon to give us a dramatic performance, usually something from one of Samuel Beckett's works. When he was finished he would call on me to sing a song, which I would do and then pass the Noble Call onto someone else in the room.

It was the last evening when Lar Burke gained star status by boldly informing the renowned Liam Clancy that interrupting a performance during a Noble Call was bad mannered and that he should know better. Mr. Clancy, in all fairness, stood corrected.

However, by that last evening of the event I was incapable of singing another note. So instead of singing I told the train story making it up as it went. Fortunately it was based on a silly joke that was told me when I was in my teens by a friend, Dennis Jones, from Tyisaf, Llanafan Fawr, and unfortunately Dennis is no longer with us. I think it surprised my audience because it was the night that I was cheered and applauded by the Stars of Ireland. Once again Liam Clancy was not going to be out done by this and opened up with a recitation of a Dylan Thomas poem in a stentorian, Burtonian voice. He had begun as we were being loaded onto the elevator at the end of the evening. He didn't stop, he continued opposite me still holding his little concertina between his hands. The man's voice echoed around the packed elevator as we descended. He was still eloquently pouring out the verses with such passion and fervor as to make a competitor in the National Eisteddfod of Wales jealous.

We reached the ground floor and the doors opened to a room full of Irish musicians who were breaking up from several music seisiuns. Liam's voice carried through the whole muddle of a crowd and it stopped them in their tracks as he delivered the last stanza. When he was finished the whole hotel erupted in a clattering applause that lasted for several minutes.

The train story has been told many times since and is often referred to by people who request it as that Go, go, go, train story. It also anchors the authors show, "John Dingley and the Biggest Pack of Lies You Ever Heard."

BIO

My earliest notion that I had realized life was wild mountains, wind sculpted hawthorn bushes, flying and singing birds, rain, with barely intermittent sunshine and mud, lots of mud. There I was in the middle of Wales, a land of song and sheep, lots of sheep.

A hill farm in Wales is an austere environment, but I loved it, no indoor plumbing or electricity. Who would care for those indoor luxuries under those clouded Welsh skies when its outdoor life enveloped you. As a child I suckled voraciously on those magnificent surroundings until the onset of adulthood.

On the hill farm I had learned many of its required trades which included milking cows morning and night. With active parents little other work remained so I apprenticed as a crystal glass cutter in my home town of Builth Wells. I became a master glass cutter and yet I was still milking my wonderful herd of dairy cows, morning and night. One day I left the crystal cutting trade and returned to the farm and more than full time work.

In 1975 to pay off family debts the farmland was sold off and I visited the land of the free and stayed longer to attend university. This was a whole new experience and again I loved it. I cut and engraved glass to help keep the proverbial wolf from the door and get me through my studies. In this other land I was ready to grasp anything that resembled home and I found it in the Irish Community of the Twin Cities.

In Wales I had been awakened to theatre when I spent some time learning with the Royal Academy of Dramatic Art and the Royal Shakespeare Theatre on one of their outreach programs in Wales, again I loved it. I performed in Wales in community theatre and then in the US I had the privilege of performing with the Na Fianna Irish Theatre and Theatre in the Round.

Because of my intense interest in wildlife conservation, and care of our planet I have, and continue to do so, serve on the board of the Raptor Resource Project where I was able to assist in the reintroduction of the Peregrine Falcon to the bluffs of the Upper Mississippi River and believe me I loved it. The Raptor Resource Project is now noted for the Decorah Eagle Cam.

Recently I helped to found the Urban Paradise Project that is busily advocating digging up those lesser used streets in cities and turning them into gardens and green recreational areas.

After years of adventures and collecting stories I have taken up writing between the many forays executing my other trade, stonemasonry. I am well on my way into a series of at least five books for children, actually for all ages, called "The Timeless Cavern" I will also be publishing shortly a nonfiction work, "Hard Work in Paradise – When all Our Food and Lives Were Organic".

Other works by John Dingley

FICTION

THE TIMELESS CAVERN (series)

Marged Evans and the Pebbles of Time (available)

Marged Evans and the Pebbles of MORE Time (available soon)

Marged Evans and the Pebbles of Distance

Marged Evans and the Pebbles of Caves

Marged Evans and the Pebbles of Space

NONFICTION

HARD WORK IN PARADISE
When All Our Food and Lives Were Organic (available soon)

MY ANIMAL ADVENTURES
A Lifetime of Animal Encounters

Reader Comments for the Midwest Book Awards finalist, THE TIMELESS CAVERN - Marged Evans and the Pebbles of Time

Enthralling! Sensational!

Just two words that I would use to describe The Timeless Cavern: Marged Evans and the Pebbles of Time.

I can't wait for Book Two! Where will Marged go next and will she be caught? *Ann Lynch*

'I thoroughly enjoyed reading this book, a fantastic story, enjoyed by myself and my children alike, a great mix of fiction and real life events, and people, we can't wait for the next instalment.' *H. M. Powell*

"The Timeless Cavern: Marged Evans and the Pebbles of Time" introduces readers to Marged Evans, a young Welsh girl who explores a mysterious cave on the edge of her family's hill farm. What she finds inside will change her life forever. A wonderful book for readers of all ages, The Timeless Cavern will be of special interest to people who enjoy time travel fantasy. I was especially intrigued by the Welsh characters and setting, although the book explores a wide variety of real and imagined characters throughout history. *Amy Ries*

If you like fiction, and are a fan of the "Harry Potter" and "Lord of the Rings" stories, this book will entertain and engage, while looking forward to the rest of the series. I personally cannot wait for Book II, "Marged Evans and the Pebbles of MORE Time"! *David L.*